W9-CRM-282

340

DISCARD

M.

AN INTRODUCTION
TO HEGEL

Oxford University Press, Amen House, London E.C. 4

EDINBURGH GLASGOW NEW YORK TORONTO MELBOURNE
WELLINGTON BOMBAY CALCUTTA MADRAS CAPE TOWN

Geoffrey Cumberlege, Publisher to the University

FIRST PUBLISHED 1940

Reprinted photographically in Great Britain
at the University Press, Oxford, from corrected
sheets of the first impression, 1948

AN INTRODUCTION TO
HEGEL

BY

G. R. G. MURE

FELLOW AND TUTOR OF
MERTON COLLEGE, OXFORD

OXFORD
AT THE CLARENDON PRESS

Stranger : O heavens, shall they easily persuade us
that absolute being is devoid of motion and life
and soul and intelligence ? That it neither lives
nor thinks, but abides in awful sanctity, mindless,
motionless, fixed ?

Theaetetus : That would be a terrible admission,
Stranger.

PLATO, *Sophist,* 248 e.

PRINTED IN GREAT BRITAIN

PREFACE

I

'A NEW idea introduces a new alternative; and we are not less indebted to a thinker when we adopt the alternative which he discarded. Philosophy never reverts to its old position after the shock of a great philosopher.' So White-head[1] refurbishes the prefatory thesis of Hegel's *Phäno-menologie des Geistes*: a philosophy is to be judged by its fruits in subsequent speculation, not merely by the polemic of direct attack and defence.

It is hard to say how Hegel emerges from either test. Controversy, it is certain, has not cleared the air; for in the hands alike of his opponents and of many sympathetic expositors he tends to become less recognizable than any other philosopher. On the other hand, perhaps the most conspicuous traces of his influence upon subsequent specu-lation are to be found in the incompatible theories of thinkers who have each borrowed some fragment of the whole Hegelian system and interpreted or reconstructed it after their own liking. Sometimes it has been the same fragment. Both dialectical materialism and less technically formulated nationalistic trends of thought owe a debt to Hegel, and it is mainly a debt to his doctrine of Objective Spirit.

The work of the British idealists and that of modern Italian philosophy have been the best products of serious effort to criticize and develop Hegel, although Hegelianism was not the sole source of either. But it must be confessed that nowhere has any thinker arisen of sufficient calibre to absorb and develop Hegel's philosophy as a whole; or to oppose Hegelianism as a whole, to grasp and embrace the entire expressed or implied alternative which he rejected. Indeed, the present state of philosophical studies is oddly desultory and miscellaneous. The plain man has never quite succeeded in seeing in the quarrels of philosophers the symptom of a free and healthy speculative activity. In that there is nothing surprising; but if he should come to suspect that philosophers are beginning to understand each other

[1] *Process and Reality*, p. 14.

so ill as to make an intelligent dispute no longer possible, then his customary charge of futility would become more difficult to answer.

II

The first English work on Hegel was not felicitously named. 'The Secret of Hegel' had an esoteric ring, and the intoxicated Carlylese in which Hutchison Stirling wrote it heightened the impression of mystery and obscured the great merits of his book. It was said that if Stirling had discovered Hegel's secret he had kept it to himself. If to-day, as I suppose is true, Hegel still seems to most philosophic students the obscurest of thinkers, the need for clarity is even greater than it was seventy years ago.

I saw little hope of lightening this darkness if I did not modify the plan usually followed in a book which professes to introduce the philosophy of a great thinker. Such a work is commonly divided into two parts. The first and smaller part is historical, while the second sets forth an outline of the system designed in itself to give the reader a bird's-eye view, and also to enable him, if he chooses, to proceed forthwith to closer study. But Hegel, as it seemed to me, demands a different treatment. In an Introduction to Hegel the initial historical portion is of dominant importance, and what is thereafter required of the writer is not so much to present a bird's-eye view as to indicate and reconnoitre—always against an historical background—the proper point of attack upon a philosophical position still not adequately located. I shall try in the next five sections to show how I conceive the historical approach, and in § viii how I understand my second duty.

III

As an historical introduction to Hegel's philosophy, it would have been a disastrous error in emphasis to offer a mere account of the general speculative outlook which held the field at the end of the eighteenth century. It is worth while to dwell a little on this point.

Hegel was born in 1770. So, incidentally, were Beethoven and Wordsworth. In the same year Kant published

his inaugural dissertation on 'The Form and Principles of
the Sensible and the Intelligible World', and Goethe was
twenty years old. Thus Hegel, who died in 1831, lived
through Germany's intellectual and artistic zenith. His
statement that he finished the *Phänomenologie* at midnight
on the eve of the battle of Jena links him significantly with
the vast and violent political changes of his time.

He was no recluse in his practical life, and no intellectual
hermit. For some years he exercised great political influence
in Prussia, and if as a philosopher he is a spectator of
eternity, yet he was also eminently a son of eighteenth- and
early nineteenth-century Germany. In his time German
culture had spread—sometimes sprawled—with burning
enthusiasm in all directions. When Hegel wrote, Goethe—
whom one of his biographers has called 'a complete civiliza-
tion in himself'—was continuing to draw poetic inspiration
from an astonishing number of sources, and to play the seer,
sometimes with considerable success, in the realms of natural
science. Hegel confessed himself Goethe's spiritual son.
Although the poet failed to make much of the philosopher's
writings, there is truth in the suggestion that Goethe's ideal
of self-culture has its philosophic implication in Hegel's
gigantic effort to penetrate the whole world of experience
with his principles; an enterprise in which he blended, one
might say, the undaunted industry of a Wagner with the
brilliant insight of a Faust, and salted the mixture with a
strong touch of Mephistophelian irony.[1] Nor was Goethe
more than perhaps the greatest of contemporary influences
upon him. A man, Hegel insists, can as soon jump out of his
skin as out of the age in which he lives, and he himself was
fired by all the divers aspirations of a great historical period.

Yet he was a stern, even a bitter critic of their more
extravagant shapes. For example, the ardour of cultured

[1]   Dann lehret man Euch jeden Tag,
         Dass, was Ihr sonst auf einem Schlag
         Getrieben, wie Essen und Trinken frei,
         Eins! Zwei! Drei! dazu nötig sei.
Hegel's answer, some thirty-five years later, to the Collegium Logicum was
his *Science of Logic*.
These reflections on Hegel and Goethe were partly suggested by Glockner;
see JE, xxi, pp. 320 ff.

Germany for Hellenism was to him a somewhat sentimental
Schwärmerei, and he was applying a needed corrective when
he called it a characteristic weakness of the age to take Plato
as its *ne plus ultra*, as the standpoint which it must assume
as its own.[1] He was not blinkered by either the eccentricities
or the archaisms of his own epoch. He knew that if all is at
some time or other contemporary, yet nothing is merely
contemporary; that if to ignore the conditions of one's time
is no path to greatness, yet to achieve greatness a man must
transform and transcend them.

The conclusion he drew was that the task of philosophy
in any age is to absorb within itself and develop the speculation of previous ages. Hegel does not, like some 'original'
thinkers, make a solitude and call it the history of philosophy. In his own lectures on that subject his great predecessors appear enhanced and not belittled. He does not
offer 'a bird's-eye view of all the ungracious past', nor
consign the *filosofica famiglia* to a limbo of hopeless desire.
His attitude to past speculation is precisely that which
Aristotle expresses in *Metaphysics A*.[2] He conceived his own
philosophy as the inheritor of past philosophies worthy of
the name, and took pains to display them as stages of a
development culminating in his own idealism. But he does
not conceive his system simply to supersede what it develops.
He thinks of it not as an Hegelianism which is not Platonism
or Aristotelianism, Spinozism or Kantianism, but as philosophy itself which now at length realizes and contains within
itself the stages of its immaturity. Hegel claims no novelty
but that of fulfilment, and is no more inspired by personal
arrogance than is Aristotle when he treats his predecessors as
'lisping' Aristotelians. If he learned from Goethe 'ein ganzer
Mensch zu sein', yet he learned it no less from Plato, and he
would not have said that the double lesson was otiose. He
is a revolutionary with his eyes fixed on the past, and if his
back is thereby turned to the future he knows at least that

---

[1] HΦ, JE, xviii, p. 178.

[2] 'Aristotle stands to the previous development of Hellenic thought in the
same relation as Hegel stands to the whole philosophical development up to
his own time, from the Hellenic, even from the Oriental world.' Croce,
What is living and what is dead in Hegel's Philosophy, Eng. tr., p. 110.

he is on firmer ground than the dreamer deluded by the vision of a new heaven and a new earth which have no rational connexion with the old.

IV

Hence to have introduced Hegel against a background consisting merely of his immediate predecessors and contemporaries would have given a most misleading impression of provincialism. Yet clearly I could not begin by outlining the whole history of philosophy as Hegel saw it, and indeed also wrote it. I had to compromise, and no doubt I shall often seem to have done so capriciously.

The first essential was to make clear Hegel's relation to Greek philosophy. For to Hegel belongs the credit of demonstrating afresh that not the flower and fruit but the entire and living root of our philosophy is still the thought of Plato and Aristotle, and that Descartes did not totally shatter the continuity of European speculation.[1] He thinks —rightly—of the Platonic and Aristotelian philosophy as one in principle. Its fundamental notion that what is most real is *eo ipso* that which is most intelligible and most good is shared by Hegel, to whom it is, in fact, the essential thesis which philosophy must make good.

Yet Hegel's debt to Plato and his debt to Aristotle are not the same; partly, perhaps, because Plato's surviving works are dialogues and those of Aristotle lecture notes. Plato's burning faith in philosophy as a life in which we have awakened from the sleep of everyday common sense and the special sciences does not recur with comparable intensity in any great philosopher before Hegel, except Spinoza. To the study of Aristotle Hegel owed, I fancy, some of his immense power to concentrate his whole thought upon the particular

---

[1] An illusion which, despite the labours of M. Gilson, seems not unlikely to recur in our own time. It is symptomatic of the present unsure historical sense in philosophy that Whitehead should observe (*Process and Reality*, p. 53) that 'The safest general characterization of the European philosophical tradition is that it consists of a series of footnotes to Plato', and yet elsewhere pronounce the dictum, 'A science which hesitates to forget its founders is lost. To this hesitation I ascribe the barrenness of logic' (cited on the title-page of Professor Stebbing's *Modern Introduction to Logic*. I have not been able to trace the reference).

issue; like Aristotle he operates always with his entire system in mind. The dialectical method shows a specially close affinity to Plato's thought, particularly in the later dialogues. But the Platonic dialogues betray trends of thought; they do not develop an explicit system. In respect of its detailed content Hegel's philosophy inevitably owes far more to Aristotle. At the beginning of the *Philosophy of Spirit*[1] Hegel remarks that the *De Anima* is still far the best, perhaps the only, work of philosophical interest on the subject; and that the main aim of a philosophy of spirit can only be to reinterpret its teaching. The same work closes with a quotation from *Metaphysics Λ.*

I was therefore bound, in introducing Hegel, to devote less space to Plato than to Aristotle, who—even apart from accidents of survival—presents classical Greek philosophy in its mature form. In Chapter X I have touched on the Platonic source of Hegel's dialectic, but I have devoted the first six chapters of this volume to Aristotle.

I offer no excuse whatever for treating Aristotle's philosophy with a certain amount of technical detail. I have never myself derived much profit from a purely general text-book sketch of any philosophy. If it is said that this book begins like a book about Aristotle and not like a book about Hegel, I can only reply that it is in design a book about both, and that I conceive the proper historical study of philosophy to be the study of at least two philosophers at once. If, on the other hand, I am charged with Hegelianizing Aristotle, I must confess that I have laid my main, though not my entire, emphasis upon what Hegel himself took to be the most important elements in Aristotle's system. But I would remind my critic that, unless both Aristotle and Hegel are hopelessly at fault, the truth of a philosophy is only to be found in those later philosophies which genuinely develop it. It is the first duty of an Aristotelian scholar to avoid anachronism, but he does not fulfil it by forgetting that the truth of any philosophy lies ahead of it. The meaning of Aristotle's statements (*a*) to himself, (*b*) to Averroes or Aquinas, and (*c*) to a modern student is by necessity not exactly the same; and the business of the modern scholar, although he can never

[1] *Enc.,* § 378.

precisely establish what Aristotle meant to Aristotle, is nevertheless to try. But his effort is simply nonsensical unless he looks for that meaning as a phase absorbed within his own conception of Aristotelianism.[1] No man—and there have been many—who professed himself a Platonist, an Aristotelian, or a Spinozist, and lived his life by the light of a long dead master's philosophy, has literally recaptured and repeated even a fragment of Plato's, Aristotle's, or Spinoza's thought. The supposition that any one could do that is as grossly absurd as its obvious corollary that the business of historical study in philosophy is to review the ages and pick out the absolutely true philosophic propositions from the totally false.

v

I did not feel justified in detaining the reader with a detailed account of more than one other predecessor of Hegel. Not unnaturally I selected Kant, and I have devoted some space, notably in Chapter IX, to the doctrines of the *Critique of Pure Reason*. I have treated Kant in more direct connexion with Hegel than I have treated Aristotle, but again I may be charged with including too many technical *minutiae*. If so, I can only repeat what I have just said about the history of philosophy.

Yet even within the scope of a necessarily narrow choice I am sensible of *lacunae*. It is the really great figures of the past who throw most light on Hegel, but an historical introduction to his work is at best over-simplified if it ignores his post-Kantian contemporaries. I have said a little of Fichte in Chapter VIII, but of Schelling almost nothing.

I have spent no more than a few sentences on modern philosophy before Kant. Of medieval thought it was less necessary to speak, although Nicolas of Cusa might well have been mentioned. A remark on Neo-Platonism would

[1] A conception of course valueless unless derived from the close study of Aristotelian texts.

Hegel makes some pertinent remarks on what the study of Greek philosophy signifies in his Preface to the second edition of the Encyclopaedia, JE, viii, p. 24. They are quoted in Wallace's *Logic of Hegel*, ed. 2, pp. xxii–xxiii.

not have been out of place, but here I feel justified in covering my lack of competence with a plea of too little space.
The omission of which I am most doubtful is that of Spinoza,
to whom Hegel owed vastly more than his critical allusions
often suggest. For Hegel's criticism of Spinoza tends to
obscure a fact which Hegel knew very well. Spinoza's
thought *is* to some extent limited and determined by its
seventeenth-century mode of expression, but very much less
so than a first reading suggests. It is less than the truth to
say, as Hegel commonly does, that Spinoza conceived spirit
only as substance and not as subject; for Spinoza himself
went far towards transcending the distinction, although he
was not in full possession of his thought. A close comparative study of Spinoza and Hegel is a task still needing to be
done. I cannot share Professor Roth's view that Spinoza
anticipates all the main doctrines of Hegel,[1] but as I rank
Plato before Aristotle so I count Spinoza a greater man than
Kant. I freely admit that by not attempting to compare him
with Hegel I have risked a failure in justice to them both.
Yet a comparison of Hegel and Kant was indispensable, and
I feared to burden the reader with a third comparative study,
which would have necessitated something of an interruption
and a fresh start.

VI

Another historical element in my introduction needs
justification. In Chapter XII I have spoken at some length
of F. H. Bradley. His philosophy, although largely inspired
by Hegel, was nevertheless a partial reaction from Hegelianism. Yet I have treated his position somewhat as a half-way
house between those of Kant and Hegel.

In the history of philosophy reaction and antecedent
approximation can never be quite the same. Had I not been
writing in England, and at a time when the political régime
in Germany affords little chance for the scholarly study of
Hegel, I should probably not have risked the dislocation
which this course entails. But in this country commentaries
on Hegel are few and mostly neither of great merit nor very
comprehensive. The average English student of Hegel is

---

[1] See 'Spinoza in Recent English Thought', *Mind*, April, 1927, pp. 206-7.

most likely to approach him directly with a background of British idealism.[1]

Moreover, the position of idealism in this country has certain native peculiarities. The British thinkers most deeply in Hegel's debt were in the main men of too much originality to exhaust their energies in direct exposition of Hegel. On the other hand, originality was not the object of their ambition. They found British philosophy in low water; clinging, smugly insular, to a native empiricism on which Hume had by implication passed sentence when he diverted his attention early in life from philosophy to history; ignoring or caricaturing the whole sweep of continental speculation which Hume's brilliant criticism had helped to stimulate. Accordingly they conceived it their business to remedy this state of barbarism by working as journeymen[2] under the shadow of German, in particular of Hegelian, philosophy.

To judge from the writings of their modern critics, it is easy to forget how great a work these journeymen accomplished. Stirling and Green and Edward Caird, Wallace and Nettleship, Bradley and Bosanquet and Joachim, were not merely the apostles of an absolutism now less fashionable than it was; they learned from Hegel to re-educate philosophic thought in their own country to that sense of historical continuity which the Englishman so easily loses when he ventures beyond practical affairs, and the German mind tends so readily to substitute for speculation. To take the most important example, no thinker since Aristotle had possessed an insight into the history of philosophy remotely comparable to Hegel's, and the Hellenism which Hegel had absorbed into his own thought was not only a vital impulse in British idealism: by linking scholarship once more with speculation, it directly stimulated a brilliant and still vigorous development of Platonic and Aristotelian studies in the

[1] Seeing the present growth of Kantian scholarship in England, this might be questioned. But I have not found in the average Kantian enthusiast much sympathy with Hegel or much knowledge of him. Rather he sees in Kant a possible last ditch against logical positivism, and at the most hopes piously to read Hegel some day when he has really mastered the first part of the *Critique of Pure Reason*.

[2] Cf. Bosanquet, *Knowledge and Reality*, p. vii.

hands of British scholars from Jowett to the present day.[1]
Yet among the better men, with the chief exception of
Wallace, these fruitful labours left little time to translate and
comment directly upon Hegel.

Moreover, despite—or perhaps because of—their great
and for a time successful efforts to make good the lag in
ideas from which their own country was suffering, the
majority of these English thinkers were markedly conserva-
tive in their idealism. The two greatest of them—the two
at any rate now regarded as most representative of their
school—were sometimes, I think, unconsciously tainted by
the very vices which they set out to attack; a not uncommon
occurrence in the history of philosophy. Bradley's tempera-
ment, if not his intellectual outlook, was perhaps rather
French than German where it was not British, and it may
be that he felt a certain distaste for alliance with German
philosophy save on his own native terms.[2] Bosanquet, a
suaver mind, was possibly too reluctant to shock, too de-
sirous to find and acknowledge the kinship between his
opponents' views and his own—British virtues less effective
in philosophical speculation than in practical life.

Yet in 1894 Bradley made an illuminating remark:

'If I had been able to keep closer to a great master like Hegel, I doubt
if after all perhaps I might not have kept nearer to the truth. . . . Even
if Hegel's construction has failed, Hegel's criticism is on our hands.
And whatever proceeds by ignoring this is likely, I will suggest, to
be mere waste of time.'[3]

Bradley was not the man to shelter behind authority, nor
was he always careful to indicate the steps by which he had
arrived at his own position, but he did not shrink from
acknowledging his debts. And Bosanquet in correspondence
was sometimes more frank than in his public writings. In
a letter to Professor Hoernlé he says of Hegel:

'To me he has not, and never had form the first, that foreignness or

---

[1] In the history of philosophy nothing has 'a merely historical interest'. Hegel
made mistakes, but it is a little laughable to hear the man mainly responsible
for a century of sympathetic and increasingly exact study of Greek thought in
Europe sneered at for a sometimes anachronistic interpretation of the pre-
Socratics.

[2] He was no doubt also influenced by Lotze's reaction from Hegel.

[3] *Collected Essays*, p. 687.

essential difficulty. Not that I can "explain" him any more than
others can, but that when I do seem to understand he speaks to me as
the only writer I can understand. What he says seems to come straight
out of one's own heart and experience; every one else seems distant
and artificial beside it.'[1]

Despite these occasional flashes of self-revelation, there
is a reserve and a reactionary element, too, in the philosophical writings of these two thinkers, which have had a
confusing effect. I have written this book partly because I
believe that there is need to make clearer to English critics
of idealism the position which they suppose themselves to
be controverting. In particular I have desired to counteract
the growing view that it is possible adequately to understand
idealist logic by studying the works of Bradley and Bosanquet in complete abstraction from Hegel.[2] I hope at least
to gain credit for a good intention.

VII

Of Hegel's life I have already said in § iii all that I mean
to say, and the question of his philosophical development I
propose to ignore. The biography of a philosopher gains
importance only so far as he fails to express himself fully in
his writings, and it then serves to explain his failure rather
than his philosophy. The half-philosopher, the empiricist
in whom the philosophic interest is never, or for a period
only, dominant, can to some extent be legitimately interpreted through the facts of his life; but the great thinker,
so far as a man may, goes whole into his thoughts. In him the
order of connexion is reversed—I might say restored—and
his philosophy explains the rest of his life.

In Hegel's case, even the history of his philosophical
development—a subject upon which he is himself, perhaps
deliberately, far from communicative—is not the primarily
important factor in grasping his thought.[3] The four major

---

[1] *Bernard Bosanquet and his Friends,* p. 116.

[2] See ch. xiii, §§ 6–6·3 below.

[3] This is not to deny that since Nohl's *Hegels theologische Jugendschriften*
(1907) much of interest has come to light through the examination of pre-
viously unpublished MSS. of Hegel. But I have ignored it, because I was sure
that any use of it would blur the broader historical outline which I have
attempted in this *Introduction.*

writings which he himself published cover a period of only
fourteen years. In the first of these, the *Phänomenologie des
Geistes*, which appeared in 1807, the essentials of his thought,
though not maturely shaped, are already present. Though
often difficult, Hegel has the huge merit of forthrightness.
He knows what he means, and he says it with vigour and
completeness of expression, and on the whole with far less
wavering and self-contradiction than most philosophers.
He published the *Encyklopaedie der philosophischen Wissenschaften* in 1817 as an authoritative compendium of his
system, and no one but himself could have produced a
summary so clear and distinct, and lacking so comparatively
little of the immense riches of Hegel's thought. The logical
doctrine contained in its first part differs in no fundamental
point from the teaching of the great *Wissenschaft der Logik*
(1812–16). The rest of it presents a Philosophy of Nature
and an outline Philosophy of Spirit which does not conflict
with the writings ampliative of its later parts, viz. the
Philosophie des Rechts (1820) and the posthumously published lectures on the Philosophy of History, Aesthetic, the
Philosophy of Religion, and the History of Philosophy.
A second edition of the Encyclopaedia in 1827 greatly ex-
panded the contents, but, with some exception in the Philosophy of Nature, made no important change of doctrine.
There are only some small further additions in the third
edition of 1830.

I have no doubt that one must assume the third edition of
the Encyclopaedia to be the authoritative outline exposition
of Hegel's philosophy. It is beyond my present purpose to
discuss the difficult question how the Philosophy of Spirit,
i.e. the Encyclopaedia outline as partially filled in by the
posthumous lectures, relates to the *Phänomenologie*. But
however this is decided, I do not myself think that the
authority of the Encyclopaedia is disturbed.

VIII

I have described the second task of an introductory work
on Hegel as consisting less in the provision of an outline
than in the attempt to disclose the true point of attack. The
close unity of form and content in Hegel's philosophy

renders any sketch of it a very bare and formal affair, but to grasp Hegel's conception of logic as the essence or the animating soul of his system—we cannot and need not here try to justify these metaphors—is the second necessary propaedeutic to detailed Hegelian studies. This is that proper point of attack. The later part of this book is therefore mainly occupied with a general contrast, in effect centring round my treatment of Bradley, between Hegel's logic and the logic of empirical thinking. The other branches of Hegel's system appear only in Chapter VIII, and only in the shape of a very slight and provisional account. The book may be found to possess some unity if it is read as a gradual approach to Hegel's conception of truth, which I have made the subject of the last two chapters.

If the general reader is disappointed, I can only regret that any project of epitomizing Hegel is delusive, and plead that the business of an Introduction is to introduce, not to provide a substitute for knowledge by acquaintance. For the professional student, and for any one else whose appetite I may be so fortunate as to have whetted, I hope very shortly to offer a book on Hegel's logic in close connexion with the present work.

IX

The use of capital letters in any work on Hegel is a hard problem. The German rule affords no clue, and English linguistic custom has long been shifting towards a more sparing use of capitals. I have accordingly tried to employ them solely in order to avoid ambiguity and not at all in order to confer dignity, confining their use, so far as I could, to the categories of Hegel's Logic and to the series of forms in his Philosophies of Nature and Spirit. Beyond that I have spelt only certain technically used words with a capital: e.g. the Absolute, Understanding, Reason, Concrete Spirit. The last-named is a term I have coined to express the province of Hegel's Philosophy of Spirit, preferring it to 'manifested spirit', a phrase which Hegel himself sometimes uses with this meaning. Spelt with a capital, 'Logic' means any author's published work on logic. In respect of Hegel it refers to the *Science of Logic* and the first part of the

Encyclopaedia taken together. I do not pretend to have escaped all anomalies or to have achieved complete consistency, but the reader will soon see how hard the decision often is.

I have included no table of Hegel's categories and forms, because I have treated them so little in detail. The reader will find a tabulation of the whole Encyclopaedia in Mr. Stace's *Philosophy of Hegel* (Macmillan), and of the *Science of Logic* in the English translation by Struthers and Johnston (George Allen & Unwin).

X

My debts are in general too great for acknowledgement, but I must record that this book would assuredly have been less bad had Harold Joachim, from whom above all men I learned such appreciation of Hegel as I possess, lived and fulfilled his promise to read in manuscript both these pages and those of the sequel I intend.

Professors J. A. Smith and Collingwood were kind enough to read the manuscript. Both have given me great help, the former, as so often before, saving me from many errors in the discussion of Aristotle. To Professor Paton I am most grateful for commenting on my treatment of Kant in Chapter IX. He enabled me to avoid at least one piece of injustice to Kant, and he warned me of other pitfalls into some of which he may think I have nevertheless tumbled through wilfulness.

G. R. G. M.

ST GERVAIS-LES-BAINS

12 *August* 1939

CONTENTS

SIGLA

JE: Jubilee reprint of the 1832–45 edition of Hegel's works, edited by Hermann Glockner; Stuttgart 1928.

Phän: *Phänomenologie des Geistes.*

LL: 'Larger Logic': *Die Wissenschaft der Logik.*

Enc: *Encyklopaedie der philosophischen Wissenschaften*, ed. 3.

EL: Part I (*Logik*) of Encyclopaedia, ed. 3.

ΦN: Part II (*Naturphilosophie*) of Encyclopaedia, ed. 3.

ΦG: Part III (*Philosophie des Geistes*) of Encyclopaedia, ed. 3.

ΦR: *Philosophie des Rechts.*

ΦH: *Vorlesungen über die Philosophie der Geschichte.*

HΦ: *Vorlesungen über die Geschichte der Philosophie.*

KRV: Kant, *Kritik der reinen Vernunft.* The first and second editions are referred to respectively as A and B, and the original paging is kept.

All references to Hegel's works are to JE (which preserves the paging of the 1832–45 edition as well as its own) unless otherwise stated.

ARISTOTLE: MATTER AND FORM, POTENTIAL AND ACTUAL

1. IT is impossible to open any philosophical discussion without a use of words too loose to satisfy even the most liberal conception of philosophic terminology.[1] We can come nearer to saying what we mean only through saying much that we do not mean. With our first sentence starts the uprush of terms equally vague and familiar. 'Universal and particular', 'real and apparent', 'content and form', 'cause and effect'; 'notion', 'idea', 'category', 'moment', 'aspect'; importantly and ineffectually they spread themselves over the page, and with them a swarm of such imprecise metaphors as commonly serve to eke them out. And though they all carry an indefinite and probably misleading suggestion of context and presupposition, they yet are from the start unavoidable.

1·1. One purpose of Hegel's Logic is to assign exact meaning to the names of all the categories of thought, not as technical terms to function indifferently in all contexts, but as meanings specialized and definite in the context of one system. Hence to make a beginning in the exposition of Hegel is particularly hard, but even in a preliminary discussion of Aristotle, which I propose, the difficulty will be already there—Aristotle was no loose user of words—and the reader must be gentle with me if I seem too often like a clumsy detective who obscures the criminal's footprints with his own. For I shall be compelled commonly to use the terminology of that elastic and hardly definable activity of mind called common sense.

1·2. Common sense *is* a rudimentary thinking—the German for it is *gesunder Menschenverstand*—but it moves most easily in the medium of sense-perception and imagination,[2] and its venture beyond these limits is never whole-hearted. It feels its thought to be a thin abstraction which

---

[1] e.g. Professor Collingwood's; cf. *Philosophical Method*, pp. 205–8.

[2] *Vorstellung*, cf. note on ch. v, § 1.

only borrows substance from the solid reality given in sense. Mostly it points and does not prove. When it passes, as it does, into natural science and mathematics it is almost, though perhaps not quite, entitled to change its name; but it never dares to believe that its own nature is revealed throughout the texture of the world it apprehends. If it did, it would no longer be common sense. Its attitude, in short, is naïvely and unreflectively realist, not a philosophical attitude. On the other hand, its language is that lowest common measure of self-expression which any philosopher, or any critic of a philosophical system, must at first adopt in order to start on terms with his reader. For at the beginning of any philosophic discussion we have hardly begun to think; we are still at a level near to sense.

It is for this reason that I shall have often to talk like a guide indicating from some point of vantage the interesting features of a landscape; I shall be compelled to speak as if the Aristotelian universe lay before us 'just so', and our task were only to see the connexions and disconnexions which it reveals to careful scrutiny.

1·3. It is indeed never possible wholly to free the language of philosophy from this more or less 'deictic' attitude, this appeal to visual imagination and to the thin abstractions which go in common sense together with it. A perfectly satisfactory philosophical terminology could only be the language of a perfectly satisfactory philosophy. Philosophical discussion, meanwhile, can never quite relinquish the undenominational medium of common-sense speech in which perforce it begins; it can never quite dispense with the current tokens of everday intercourse, minted in the expression of all kinds of emotion, but hacked and rubbed by convention to roughly homogeneous meanings in the communication of non-philosophical interests. It may be that, as Aristotle says, we cannot think without imagery; but thought is not imagination, nor is it a tenuous abstraction from sense. Hegel taught no more important lesson than this, nor one more seldom learnt.

It therefore needs a constant self-discipline on the part of a philosophical writer, and his reader's alert co-operation, if they are together to escape the error from which all sham philosophy springs. The writer must gradually reshape his terminology, and the reader must watch the transformation. Moreover the transformation can never be complete, and every introduction of a relatively new topic entails a relatively new beginning at a level near to sense.

2. It may be said quite generally[1] that Aristotle inherited from Plato, and accepted without question, the conception of the universe as a single hierarchy of stages wherein each higher stage stands related to the stage beneath it as the more perfect and developed to the less perfect and developed. The peak of this hierarchy, inasmuch as it is fully perfect, is fully real, fully intelligible, and wholly exempt from change—though not therefore static.[2] The base of it is a series of stages which together constitute an imperfect world of perceptible things which change, and are not real at any rate as the highest stage is real. Between base and peak there are many intermediate stages.

2·01. The term 'real' in this context must be understood as translating either τὸ ἀληθές or τὸ (ὄντως) ὄν. It means in Plato and Aristotle—and this, indeed, is in the last resort its only possible meaning—the opposite of the sham. It is that which actually does possess the nature which it claims, or which is claimed on behalf of it. We shall see later the immense importance of this doctrine, which Hegel accepts as a matter of course.

2·1. The *Scala Naturae* begins to show definite features when we examine the nature of change. Although a changing perceptible thing is in a certain sense not fully real nor intelligible, yet change is not wholly irrational. It seemed to Aristotle that the Platonic triune norm of reality, intelligibility, and value[3] is reflected far more clearly than Plato had observed in the nature of change, which at first sight appears to contradict it. The terminals of any process of change are opposites, and all change is change for the better or for the worse. That is to say change is development

---

[1] The following sketch is in the main an abbreviation—with, however, some difference of emphasis—from my *Aristotle*. I have therefore been sparing of references to Aristotle's works.

[2] Cf. Plato, *Sophist*, 248 E, quoted on title-page.

[3] In the sense of goodness. See Preface, p. vii.

from a less perfect, real, and intelligible condition of the changing thing towards a more perfect, real, and intelligible condition, or vice versa. Two simple and fairly typical examples are (i) the development from fertilized ovum to adult in all animals, and their decline from maturity through old age to dissolution; (ii) the process of artificial construction, as when a sculptor works up a mass of bronze into a finished statue, which he can, if he wishes, then melt down again into a formless lump.

2·2. To say that all change is development[1] and is rational is to say that it has a cause; for to Aristotle knowledge is knowledge of a cause or reason. To understand Aristotle's very broad notion of cause, as the answer to all questions which can properly be asked about the coming to be and being of anything, is indispensable to any student of European philosophy. But his notion of cause is based on his view that any perceptible changing thing is a composite of matter and form. Hence the contrast of matter and form has first to be examined.

Speaking quite generally, 'matter' means the materials out of which a thing is constituted; 'form' is the structure which unifies the materials into a single whole. The bronze is the matter of the statue; its shape—a precise scheme of quantitative relations, a proportion which is quantity passed over into quality—is its form. The flesh, blood, bones—all the various tissues and organs—are the matter of the living animal. The unifying form, however, of the animal is a unity not merely of proportioned structure: it is the peculiar unity of operations which characterizes an animal as such, a special sort of life.

Matter is thus not the solid abiding 'stuff' of the classical physicists' atom; not what Dr. Johnson thought he was kicking when he 'refuted' Berkeley. Matter is never matter in its own right: it goes with form to constitute a pair of strictly correlative terms.

There is no perceptible thing which cannot be analysed into matter and form.[2]

---

[1] i.e. is a passage between worse and better in some sense of the terms. Even locomotion is no exception; see ch. ii, § 5·3 below.

[2] And also much that is not merely perceptible can be so analysed.

2·3. But perceptible things are changing things, and this analysis into matter and form reveals merely the non-transient factor or 'moment' of change, merely displays the thing as static. It is only by, as it were, mentally arresting the stream of development or decay at a given instant that we can show the thing as a concrete of matter and form. We have still to ask what happens to this balance of matter and form when the thing changes. The answer is that the balance also changes. If we take, so to speak, a cinematographic film of the thing actually developing instead of a snapshot, it will show an increasing preponderance of form and a decreasing degree of matter. As the statue realizes its shape the bronze becomes less and less formless, less and less *merely* bronze. During the animal's growth its organs become less and less *mere* matter as they come gradually to be informed by the perfected structure and function which characterize the mature animal.

2·4. It is important to observe—though difficult to express—that in this process change is not predicable of either matter or form, but only of the concrete thing. It is the whole composite which comes to be, or comes to be different from what it was. Matter in general and form in general do not change, any more than change itself changes. We can legitimately speak of the bronze of the statue and of the animal's organs as changing only in so far as we take them as already concretes of matter and form.[1]

2·5. The truth of this becomes more evident when Aristotle proceeds to interpret further the fluctuating balance of matter and form in the changing thing. He holds that matter and form kinetically viewed are respectively potentiality and actuality. In its change the thing, which statically considered is a concrete of matter and form, unites the two factors or moments of potentiality and actuality: in fact, so far as the thing is a changing thing it *is* their union.

This union is imperfect and unstable because the thing is imperfect, but Aristotle implies that it is really less true to call the thing a concrete of matter and form than to call it a

Aristotle's is no mere dualist doctrine of a material and a spiritual world defined as positive opposites.

[1] i.e. *proximate* matters; see § 2·61 below.

union of potential and actual. The second definition includes the first. For only that which changes can ever be in a static condition: that which is exempt from change because it is superior to change is not, in Aristotle's view, static. Change for Aristotle is always development. The changing thing retains its self-identity through a transience, or passage, which presupposes but cancels its static condition.[1] Hence the static analysis into matter and form, while it prefigures and is presupposed in the fuller analysis, is, if taken by itself, an abstract account of that reality which the thing possesses. The thing of the perceptible world is a *changing* thing: imperfect as it is, it would not be more real if it ceased for ever to alter. Hence to call it a concrete of matter and form is to call it less than it is; to call it an unstable union of potential and actual is to name it more truly because more fully.

2·6. The close connexion of these two analyses is obvious when we examine more nearly the claim of any changing thing to be taken as real.

If we think in terms of matter and form we must say that in every concrete the form is the real and intelligible factor. It is the shape of the statue which makes it what it really is; it is its peculiar unity of vital functions, its ψυχή, 'soul' or 'life-principle', which makes the animal an animal. These are what we must grasp if we would understand the statue and the animal and not merely perceive them with the senses. Definition must be in terms of form, and the material factor is subservient to the form: it exists only in order to be the 'medium' or 'vehicle' of the form. It is indispensable to its concrete, but it is as such not intelligible or real.

2·61. This at first sight may not seem obvious. It may be objected that the bronze is itself something real and intelligible; that one understands not the mere shape of the statue but the bronze and the shape as two positive constituents in mutually complementary union. But to say so is to forget that every perceptible thing can be analysed into matter and form, and that the analysis will therefore apply just as well to the original mass of bronze as to the finished statue. The mass of bronze is a form—in this case a certain structural principle, a certain precise quantitative formula—

[1] As Kant puts the paradox, 'only the permanent changes'.

which so combines and unifies a matter consisting of simpler physical constituents that they make bronze and not some other thing. The analysis can then be applied to these simpler constituents, which in fact Aristotle believed to be earth, water, air, and fire. And if we press the analytic process still further down, we are bound to meet, as the ideal lower limit of the whole developing series of information, a primary matter which is utterly devoid of form. Of this matter change is not predicable. It is nothing actually existent. But it is at least a logical postulate of the development.

Such is the peculiar and ambiguous nature of matter, and it follows that, though in any concrete thing matter and form appear to be two positive factors which complement one another, yet really the matter of the concrete gets its apparently positive character only in virtue of form, and is *per se* purely negative.[1] It is only the *proximate* matter—the immediately preceding stage of the developing thing—which has the appearance of being a positive constituent, and this proximate matter is an already informed matter. Ultimately —*en fin de compte*—a perceptible thing is real (actual) only so far as it is informed.

It is thus that Aristotle comes to treat matter and form as merely the static and less complete aspects of the potential and the actual. So far as a thing is undeveloped it *is* only potentially (δυνάμει), which means that it is more matter and less form; so far as it is developed it *is* actually (ἐνεργείᾳ), i.e. it is more form and less matter.

2·7. An obvious corollary follows. If there be an entity wherein no residue of matter and potentiality persists, it will be not a perfectly harmonized concrete of matter and form but pure form and actuality. Pure form and actuality will in fact be the final term in the developing scale of which primary matter was the starting-point. But it will not be merely a logical postulate: it will be the only thing ultimately real and intelligible and good.

[1] Cf. Averroës: 'Materia dicitur quod habet esse de eo quod sibi advenit, quia de se habet esse incompletum, immo nullum esse habet.'

ARISTOTLE : CAUSATION

1. ARISTOTLE's theory of cause, which we are now better equipped to consider, is a fourfold analysis. It is the further elaboration and development of the two analyses which we have already discussed. We have seen that the developing thing is real and intelligible just so far as it is informed and actual, whereas so far as it is merely material and potential it is not real and not intelligible, but only perceptible. If we only know when we know the cause,[1] it follows that cause is form and actuality; and that is the gist of Aristotle's teaching.

2. In the perceptible world, where the thing we strive to know is a developing thing, the cause whereby we know it is fourfold. The *formal cause* of the thing is the form which informs it more or less completely according to the degree to which the thing is developed and perfected. The formal cause, for example, equally of the fertilized ovum, the embryo, and the adult animal is that specific animal form which the animal will embody when it reaches maturity. The only *positive* definition which can be given of a child—or indeed of a human foetus—is a definition in terms of adult manhood. To that the definer can only add that the child or the foetus is *not yet* a man. Positive definition of a singular developing thing must be in this sense proleptic, for the reality of a thing and the clue to its meaning lie in its developed structure, not in its simple unintegrated elements. It expresses and reveals itself at its climax and not in its origin.[2] It must be defined, so to speak, *sub specie superioris* and not *sub specie inferioris*.[3]

---

[1] Cf. ch. i, § 2·2, but also § 6·1 of this chapter.

[2] How this doctrine, which begins with Plato and probably Socrates, reverses the attitude of earlier Greek philosophy, I have tried to show in an article entitled *Change*, published in *Philosophy*, April and July 1934.

[3] It may seem plausible to retort, 'Why not define the thing as it stands, i.e. on the level at which you find it?' But a singular perceptible thing cannot be so defined, if for no other reason because the proposed definition would exclude from the *definiendum* the course of change which is essential to its nature. *Any* definition must transcend the immediate presentation of the

3. If there be a perfect and fully real thing, it is *causa sui* and cannot be *analysed* in causal terms. But the thing which we are trying to know in the perceptible world is a developing thing. Hence its form, though constituting the sole criterion for defining it, is at the same time an unactualized ideal which lies beyond it so long as it is not fully developed, and behind it so soon as it begins to decline. In the one case the thing does not yet conform, in the other it has ceased to conform, to its own real nature. In so far as this is so its form is operant *a fronte* as its *final cause*; the unreached goal of its development; that perfection for the sake of which it is developing, or, in Aristotle's precise words, 'that for the sake of which [*sc.* it is and develops], i.e. its good'.

4. Its form is thus that which gives to the developing thing what reality it has, and it is also that perfection which the thing is tending to realize. But since form causes the being of a thing, and since the thing is also a developing thing, it follows further that only form can set in motion this development towards the thing's own actual nature. In this new role form is *efficient cause*. The efficient cause is embodied in another existent separate from the changing thing. It acts upon the latter *a tergo* and in a relatively external manner: its action is transeunt, not immanent.

5. It is worth while pausing to illustrate briefly these three factors revealed by causal analysis before we examine the fourth factor in the process.

In the world of animate Nature the formal cause of any developing thing, vegetable or animal, is its specific form, the distinctive character of its species, which the specimen will embody adequately when it is full grown. This too is its final cause, that consummation for the sake of which it grows.[1] The efficient cause of its coming to be and growing is the specific form embodied in the adult parent; in the case of the animal its male parent. That is, puberty marks the climax of growth, at which the specific form is attained by the specimen.

definiendum in sense-perception. The attempt to define things (perceptible or otherwise) 'as they stand' usually leads to a doctrine of '*in*definables' and 'not further analysables'.

[1] In Nature final cause is not conscious purpose, but the goal of what may be called a 'nisus' or a 'tendency' according to the level at which it operates.

5·1. In the conscious purposive process of moral will form is most conspicuous as final cause; i.e. as the ideal end or plan present in the mind of the agent but not yet actualized. In so far, moreover, as this ideally conceived end is *only* ideal, the object of unsatisfied desire and so discrepant with the actually present situation, it is also that which impels the agent here and now to act: it is the efficient cause, father to the act. And further—though the sense of struggle, the complication and chaotic diversity of particular human ends, may hide the truth both from the agent himself and from the superficial philosopher—yet here too form is formal cause. No doubt the child (many adult children too) takes on trust from his pastors and masters a rule of sound conduct which operates in his behaviour as a relatively external efficient cause, and to him the end then appears more or less alien and possibly repugnant. But the mature moral agent has become his own master and himself embodies the rule. His conduct is autonomous. He neither takes another man's word nor blindly obeys an unexplained imperative which dictates a miscellany of detached duties. He does his duty because he knows himself. The end which he actualizes, his good, belongs essentially to the distinctive nature of man as that is individualized in his own peculiar nature as an agent. Certainly the nisus in the moral agent towards his end is difficult to characterize. The good moves him, itself unmoved. Yet this motivation of his action is not an 'impulsion', nor even an 'attraction', by something external to himself.[1] For the agent in his action realizes—unless he perverts[2]—the human nature which makes him what he is, as truly as a plant matures towards the specific form in terms of which it is to be defined. Moreover, because human nature, so far at least as it is practical, is essentially social—not merely and barely gregarious but self-differentiating in communal life—the good in which he realizes himself is a common good.

5·2. Change in the practical arts (from which Aristotle,

---

[1] For the ultimate problem here involved see ch. vi below.
[2] Aristotle holds that the end of any action must at least appear good to the agent. Evil—man's realization of his capacities in perverse action—is beyond the scope of this sketch; see my *Aristotle*, pp. 148–9.

like Plato, fails to distinguish effectively the fine arts) is
analogous to conduct in that it exhibits the same triune
form. The ideally conceived shape of the artefact is final and
efficient cause in the artist's process of making, at once the
aim and the stimulus. Inasmuch as the purpose of any art
is a subordinate element within, or at any rate a phase of
activity subservient to, the whole moral plan of life, the form
is also formal cause. On the other hand, although the artist
does thus actualize and express himself in his product, yet
he does so in a more external manner than the moral agent:
he does not, like the latter, directly fashion himself. Moreover in art the relation of form to matter is also relatively
external. The artist's materials are final products of Nature,
and their subsequent alteration by man is therefore a development comparatively unessential to them. It is, in
Aristotle's terminology, a change of quality and not of substance. Art is thus an intermediate phase which links conduct with the unconscious teleological working of Nature.

5.3. On the inanimate levels of Nature form already
operates in these three causal aspects. An illustration, which
wears perhaps nowadays an archaic air, is the Aristotelian
theory of gravity and natural place, according to which
earth in tending to fall is seeking its true station in the sublunary sphere, and completes its proper nature in attaining
it. But the same doctrine appears in Aristotle's acute account
of motion which is compulsory and not natural. When a
physical body is moved by compulsion, a second impelling
body is the proximate cause. In the sphere of action final
cause was dominant, but here efficient—and therefore external and transeunt—operation is the conspicuous aspect
of causality. Yet when a body is moved there are realized in
it (and together they constitute a *single* actualization) (i) the
impelling body's potentiality of imparting motion, and (ii)
its own potentiality of being moved. Moreover the impelled
body then first acquires the capacity of imparting motion to
a third body. Thus although compulsory motion is initiated
in the last resort by something which is not a physical body,
yet even in the handing on of this 'unnatural' movement
from one physical body to another something like formal
and final cause is operative. The distinction between natural

and compulsory movement turns out after all to be not absolute.

5·4. The lowest level of natural change in the sublunary physical world is a ceaseless cyclical transformation of earth, water, air, and fire into one another. These are the simplest physical bodies, and analysis reveals in each of them only a pair of the contrary 'qualities' hot and cold, dry and fluid; 'qualities' which are really mere *qualia* below any distinction of thing and quality. Below these contraries is nothing but primary matter. But even at this lowest level of incontinent transformation form fulfils obscurely its threefold function. There is an order of fineness in the elements,[1] and change is for the better or the worse.

5·5. Thus change at every level of the changing world is in some degree spontaneous. Everywhere it is at least a development which expresses some urge or tendency analogous to conscious purpose. Freedom dwindles as the scale is descended, but it does not wholly vanish. The changing thing is always in some measure self-changed: its own nature moves it even where we seem to detect nothing beyond quite external efficient causation or mere incontinent collapse into another nature.

6. The fourth factor which all causal analysis reveals is the *material cause*. Matter as a fourth aspect of causation is of course not a fourth aspect of form. Yet it is not a cause deriving from another source. It is a necessary but passive condition of development. It is that out of which a thing develops and that into which it dissolves, and it is a substratum receptive of form and persisting throughout change. Aristotle holds that a thing also, though incidentally, comes to be out of its 'privation' (the determinate absence of its form) as out of its contrary. The substratum, the thing's nature as the determinable of the process, has thus a negative as well as a positive moment: matter, i.e., is also the residue of mere potentiality which dwindles in the course of development, but never quite disappears in the world of change. As such, it is the negative addition to positive definition which we make by saying that the *definiendum* is not yet fully

---

[1] Cf. I am fire and air; my other elements
I give to baser life.

actualized. Since nothing in the world of change is fully real, definition even of the mature thing does in principle require this addition.[1] In every thing of the perceptible world matter plays this ambiguous role: there is no perfect specimen, no pure case of any natural species. If positive definition of the immature specimen can only be proleptic,[2] positive definition even of the mature specimen can only be approximative.

6·1. In short, matter is both a cause of a thing's being and *the* cause of its not-being. In Chapter I, §§ 2·5 ff., where the relation of potential and actual to matter and form was discussed, I may have seemed uncandid in emphasizing the negative rather than the positive moment of matter. It was in fact because I believed it the harder aspect to grasp that I there exhibited potentiality rather as a fuller characterization of matter *qua* privation than of matter *qua* positive substratum. But the positive, or *quasi*-positive, factor of matter is not to be ignored, as Aristotle indicates by dignifying it with the name of cause. And potentiality, too, has its corresponding positive moment: the fuller characterization of matter *qua* positive substratum is 'capacity' or 'potency', the real, though unrealized, promise of actuality. Hence the reason why proximate matter appears to be a positive complement of form[2] is that proximate matter is also and further the positive potency of actualization in and as the form to which it is proximate.[3]

And so the corollary pointed out in Chapter I, § 2·7, also requires restatement: an entity without residue of potentiality will be not merely pure actuality but, also and further, pure activity.

7. Hence my attempt in Chapter I, § 2·61, to meet the possible objection that matter is a positively contributory constituent of any concrete by showing that matter reduces on resolute analysis to no more than an utterly formless and indeterminate primary matter, and that form alone contributes the real and intelligible nature of a thing, did not quite

---

[1] Cf. § 2 above.   [2] See ch. i, § 2·61 above.

[3] It is fatally easy at any level to go further and fall into the error of treating its proximate matter as the whole nature of a concrete, thus contenting oneself with an explanation of form in terms of matter.

fairly and fully meet the difficulty. For in matter even thus apparently shorn of all positivity—tracked to its source and found harmlessly null—lurks the problem to which speculation returns as the tongue to the aching tooth. Primary matter, it was said, is at least a logical postulate of development. That would seem to imply that the strict correlates, matter and form, *together* constitute a principle; are a dual category of coupled moments in terms of which we are bound to think the world of change.[1] But only form, we also said, is intelligible, and so is opposed to matter, which as such defies the intelligence; and in that case a divorce threatens between the intelligible and the real, although their union is a fundamental tenet of Platonic and Aristotelian—and indeed of Hegelian—philosophy.

7·1. Many thinkers have professed themselves undisturbed by this conclusion; holding that the real and the intelligible do not necessarily coincide, and perhaps maintaining that insistence on their coincidence must in the end falsify such knowledge as we do possess of the world in which we live. That is a view which probably from time to time any open-minded thinker finds forcibly returning on him; but, unless it eventually shuts his mind, he also discovers that with every recurrence its difficulty grows greater. Here be it only said that when a real but unintelligible matter is opposed to real and intelligible form, *both* terms of the relation are presumably implied to be understood, and in order to characterize matter we have then to coin some such self-contradictory phrase as 'alogical principle'. For if matter is *per se* unintelligible, nothing true or false can be said about it, and it is in fact only in opposition to, and in correlation with form that we have been tempted to call it unintelligible.

Nevertheless, if in any sense the intelligible can be said to include within itself the unintelligible, we are as yet in no position to say what that sense is. We have not yet even asked what intelligence is, nor inquired into the nature of its categories. We have now to examine a little more closely the Aristotelian universe which we have begun to develop

---

[1] It is significant that Aristotle treats the relation of genus to species as one of matter to form; cf. below, ch. iv, § 1·2.

through the three stages of analysis, viz. matter and form, potential and actual, and finally cause. At present we must provisionally accept the ambiguous nature of matter as a *de facto* characteristic which somehow signalizes the relative unreality of the world of change.

III

ARISTOTLE: THE *SCALA NATURAE*

1. The transmutation of the four sublunary elements takes place within a nest of concentric aetherial spheres, to whose eternal revolutions their ceaseless cyclical transformation is due. When the transformation is incomplete there emerge relatively stable compounds of the four elements, but there remains always a large residue of uncompounded earth, water, fire, and air. These compounds are the minerals, and also the various vegetable and animal tissues—bark, sap, flesh, blood, &c. They differ specifically from one another according to the proportion in which the four elements are compounded in them. This proportion is the form of the compound, and it is present in the smallest physically separable fragment of each specimen.

2. The tissue-compounds unite in a new type of combination to constitute the organs of a living body. The form of an organ is too complex to be revealed in the separate fragment. The term 'organ' (instrument) is significant: the 'purpose' of matter to subserve form is becoming explicit. For these organs next combine as proximate matter for yet higher principles of information, which may be called forms of organization. This is the level of vegetable life. If we analyse a plant into matter and form, its matter is its ordered group of instrumental organs, its form is its characteristic triune life-function of assimilating nourishment, growing, and reproducing its kind. Its matter has a very positive appearance, but only because it is an already highly elaborated form, and it quite obviously exists only to subserve form.

The distinctive vegetable form, then, is not a mere chemical formula such as turns the four elements to gold instead of granite, or to sap instead of silver. It is an operation, or rather a graded unity of operations: the form of a vegetable is its life. The special significance of this new stage of form is marked by the thoroughness with which it penetrates—or, more accurately, absorbs and transcends—the three proximately lower stages. Tissues, organs, and the bodies they compose never exist independently; and once life is extinct, they are, even in the case of a plant, nothing whatever but chemical compounds.

3. Again ascending the scale, we find that this assimilative and reproductive principle, with all the various stages which it contains modified and transcended, has become matter to the fresh form of animal life. An animal eats, grows, and reproduces its kind, but in the animal these functions are matter and instrument to a higher form. The essential unity of functions which informs an animal is the scarcely divided activity, or *quasi*-activity, of sense and appetition. An animal's nutritive and reproductive make-up is necessary to it, but only as a proximate matter subserving that sentient-appetitive function which is the true animal form. Hence the vegetable functions of an animal are greatly modified from those of a plant. In particular they are intermittent.

4. The final stage in the sublunary world is the human species. The distinctive defining form of this is the rational soul of man, wherein animal sentience and appetite, with all the lower stages of information which have culminated in them, are once again a proximate instrumental matter subserving a new unity of soul-functions.[1]

In a brute animal sentience and appetition are scarcely separate. In man development from this common root is a partial bifurcation entailing frequent conflict. The plant maintains a tranquil life and decays, or it is eaten and digested into animal tissue. The animal perceives, feels pleasure and pain, and seeks and shuns accordingly. But man is at times in conscious struggle with himself. Moreover he is not merely practical. In man there develops from sense-perception a cognitive activity which he exercises for its own sake. In Chapter II, §§ 5 and 5·1, we caught a glimpse of Aristotle's interpretation of the will in art and conduct, and something must later be said of thought. Meanwhile we must pause to notice rather carefully his doctrine of sense-perception, which shows an especially close affinity with Hegel,[2] and then turn back to review the stages of the *Scala Universi* which we have so far climbed.

---

[1] The Aristotelian term ψυχή covers 'life', 'soul', and 'mind'.
[2] Cf. Hegel, HΦ, JE, xviii, pp. 376 ff.

4·1. The physical conditions of an act of sense-perception are a physical body, an organ (if we take sight as typical, an eye), and a medium. These must all have certain properties in common. Something which Aristotle calls 'transparency' is present in the physical body and the eye in the form of colour—indeed transparency in the form of colour is present on the surface of any definitely bounded body. The transparency of bodies such as air and water, which have no definite bounding surface, has, when actualized (e.g. by fire), the form of light. Light is thus the medium of vision. Colour in the physical thing stimulates a change in light, and, mediately, in the eye.

4·2. If we now pass above this purely physical level, at which Aristotle's theorizing is ingenious if obsolete, and at least not much less successful than that of modern physiology in explaining the instrumental function of matter in awareness, we find a highly suggestive doctrine of the concrete act of sense-perception, which is vital to the comprehension of Hegel.

In examining this we must bear vividly in mind the truth that the physical factor is now a proximate matter subserving a higher form. Aristotle has expressed himself in a simile which has lamentably misled generations of empiricists.[1]

'A sense', he says,[2] 'is that which is receptive of sensible forms without their matter, as wax takes on the device of the signet-ring without the iron or the gold; it takes on the golden or the bronze device, *but not qua golden or of bronze.* Correspondingly, in the perception of each sensible, the sense is acted on by what is coloured or flavoured or sounding *not in so far as each of these sensibles is called a particular thing but in so far as it is of a certain kind, i.e. in respect of its definable form.*'

The words which I have italicized show that no crude copy theory is intended. Doubtless there is, on Aristotle's theory, a physical alteration in the organ, but that is (*a*) not a static print or image but a process, and (*b*) not for a moment supposed by Aristotle to be in itself the complete act of sense-perception. To interpret literally the signet-ring simile is to explain sense-perception in terms of a purely *a tergo* effi-

---

[1] And even, I think, Leibniz; cf. *Nouveaux Essais*, Preface, Gerhardt's ed., vol. v, p. 42.

[2] *De Anima*, 424ª 17 ff.

cient causation, and barbarously to mutilate the Aristotelian theory of cause. The real purpose of the simile is to show that in sense-perception the universal is already present in a rudimentary phase.[1]

4·3. The full meaning of that remark is still far to seek, but Aristotle's further teaching yet more plainly forbids any literal interpretation of his simile. In the act of sense-perception two potentialities are actualized, a capacity in the sensible object and a capacity or potency in the percipient. But their actualization is a single actualization, and it takes place wholly in the percipient. Moreover the actualization of capacity on the part of the object is a communication to the percipient of the object's essential form, not the actualization of a mere capacity to stimulate which in being actualized leaves the stimulating object unaffected in its own nature.

4·4. This is clear if we compare the act of perception with one of its lower analogues. When a moving body strikes and imparts compulsory motion to a stationary body,[2] the patient's capacity for being moved and the agent's capacity for moving are together singly actualized in the patient. But the patient then merely takes on the nature of the agent without developing it. Save so far as approach to, or removal from, its proper station is also involved, the impelled body merely repeats the motion of the impelling body. For the two bodies are as nearly *in pari materia* as two terms in a process of change can be. But the case of sense-perception is different. The object in its perceptible character—its colour, or its sonority, or its hardness—constitutes together with the organ's capacity to see, or hear, or touch, the proximate matter of a qualitatively new information. It fulfils its nature in the concrete act of sense-perception, for the sake of which it exists.[3]

---

[1] A doctrine that sense is literally impressed by 'external' things might be held compatible with the crude representative theory of judgement which Aristotle expands in *De Interpretatione* and implies in the *Categories*. But these are most probably early works, and any such interpretation of the signet-ring simile in its context in the mature *De Anima* is patently absurd.

[2] See ch. ii, § 5·3 above.

[3] The assimilation of food (an assimilation both of form and matter) is an intermediate type of change.

4·5. This theory is not without gaps and ambiguities. The matter of the single perceptive act combines two elements which seem to be stages on two different scales of information, the connexion of which is not adequately explained. (*a*) The *substrata* of perceptible qualities, the not actually perceived perceptibles, are said by Aristotle to exist apart from the act of sense-perception: he does not teach a naïve subjective idealism.[1] (*b*) The organ too, though even apart from its acts of perceiving it is at a higher level of information than the unperceived perceptible, and though in the act of its own perceptive function it is not a part of the object perceived, is nevertheless a perceptible physical thing. Thus at first sight it looks as if Aristotle were naïvely positing two juxtaposed sets of 'realistic' things, of which the one set stimulates the other to perceive it. But the perceptible is only and necessarily *actualized* in being perceived: its actual, though not its potential, *esse* is *percipi*. Therefore there can be no inference to the nature of any sort of physical thing in a world supposed indifferent to a subject's consciousness; Aristotle clearly excludes any naïvely realist view of the object of the perceptive act. But he does on the other hand appear naïvely to presuppose the organ. The perceptible physical characters of the organ, however, can be no more independent of consciousness than those of the object which stimulates it.[2]

4·6. A few further points are worth remarking. A special sense in grasping a special sensible is said by Aristotle to be infallible. This is not the germ of a modern realist theory of *sensa*. The infallibility is below the level of truth and falsehood; it is a hint of the mere sensation, neither truly active nor truly passive, which sense-perception presupposes. Aristotle never clearly distinguishes sheer sensation from sense-perception, but he holds quite clearly that sense-perception is essentially a discriminative capacity, and that the special senses never in fact operate as isolated functions. Even in perceiving its peculiar simple perceptible—colour,

---

[1] cf. HΦ, JE, xviii, pp. 376–8 and 381, where Hegel contrasts Aristotle with Leibniz and Fichte.

[2] The medium is a further naïve presupposition: light, for example, is itself perceptible.

sound, odour, &c.—a sense is special because the general
activity of *sensus communis* is operative in its specialized
function.

4·7. The relation of *sensus communis* to the five senses is
interesting and important. Aristotle grades the latter hierarchically at least to the extent of regarding touch as the
lowest and the presupposition of the rest, hearing and sight
as the highest. To *sensus communis* he ascribes a fourfold
power. (1) It appears in all specialized operation of sense
as the self-consciousness which accompanies the latter as a
sort of by-product. I see and also perceive that I see, &c.
(2) It discriminates between two qualities perceived at the
same time by one sense, and between the objects of two
senses. (3) Certain characters—time, change and quiescence,
number and unity, figure, and magnitude—are common to
all perceived physical bodies. They are perceived in the
exercise of more than one special sense, but only incidentally. Essentially they are perceived by *sensus communis*
specialized in sight and touch.[1] (4) When we perceive in the
object any other character which is only incidental to the
special sense which we are exercising, the perception of it
is due to *sensus communis*.

Thus sense does not conform to Aristotle's official conception of a genus of co-ordinate species.[2] *Sensus communis*
is not exhaustively differentiated in the functions of the five
senses. But it is not a sixth special sense, and its peculiar
contribution to sense awareness is not the fruit of separate
exercise. Rather it is at once a crown of the hierarchy of the
five senses and at the same time the common nature graded
and differentiated in them.

4·8. The main defects, then, in this account of sense
appear to be (1) its neglect of the fact that discriminative
sense-perception arises out of what may be called by contrast sheer sensation; (2) its assumption of perceptive organs
and media which in fact owe their status to sense-perception:
that is, Aristotle tries to explain sense-perception within a
setting which contains an element already itself presupposing sense-perception.

---

[1] Aristotle sometimes adds the other senses.
[2] Cf. ch. iv, § 2 below.

5. The latter point raises the problem of distinguishing between the special natural sciences and a philosophical interpretation of Nature; a distinction not in itself easy, never quite clear in Aristotle, and of great importance for the understanding of Hegel. At the risk of wearying the reader I venture to offer some mainly anticipatory remarks.

To put the matter first from the point of view of natural science. Biologists commonly find themselves in this dilemma. If they adopt a vitalist position and openly treat the organism as functioning teleologically, they have then to explain the relation of animate patches of Nature to an inanimate environment which is assumed to behave mechanically. But animate and inanimate are not *in pari materia*, and the principle of relation between them has to be borrowed either from the one or the other. Either the animate must be held to effect a partial transformation into its own nature of a mechanical system; or else animate and inanimate must be held to interact, or to be related by some other such mechanical relation. But the first solution is sheer appeal to miracle, while if a mechanical relation be introduced teleology is put wholly out of court, and the organism is simply dissolved into its mechanical environment.

The only possible line of solution, as it seems, is to regress upon the assumption which begets the dilemma; to deny that animate and inanimate can be interpreted at all as juxtaposed patches related on the same level; to maintain that Nature *qua* environment of organism must from the start within biology be *in pari materia* with, enter into the life of, organism.[1]

For Aristotle the problem is a little different, because he is nowhere content to dispense altogether with teleological explanation; for him the environment is never sheerly mechanical. Yet even if Aristotle does take the environment everywhere as itself teleological system, yet he does not display it as *in pari materia* with the living organism: the ends served remain on different levels and partly heterogeneous.

5·1. To the student of psychology as a special science the relation of consciousness to mere life offers an analogous problem. But in his case the difficulty is most obvious when

[1] Even if biological interpretation of Nature as a whole is still in its infancy.

he ignores the intervening level of life and tries to relate the sense-percipient to the object-world of his perception. Here, when we substitute consciousness for life, the old dilemma recurs, and just because the intermediate level of life is ignored, it is more painful.

Once again the line of solution seems to be the same; although, if we are to ignore the fact that what the percipient perceives he also lives, it can only be expressed in an over-simplified form. The *perceptum* must be *in pari materia* with the percipient; otherwise sense-perception is either a miracle or nothing but a mechanically determined event. This is not to say that percipients perceive nothing but percipients, but that the world *qua* object of perception enters into the nature of the percipient. Percipient consciousness, as we shall find Hegel to have discovered, is nothing less than the whole concrete attitude of percipient to perceived object. To be a percipient is essentially to be a centre or a focus of a world. We are far too apt to think of minds, and even of organisms, as maintaining themselves in an alien and indifferent physical universe by a sort of precarious squatter's right. We forget that what we are then doing is to make a quite illogical addition of heterogeneous elements to the hypothetical world of the more abstract natural sciences, a world which, quite properly, excludes life and mind.

5·2. In short, alike for the biologist and the psychologist the problem defies solution so long as the universe we experience is assumed to be, as J. S. Haldane puts it,

'made up of a scattered picture in which we find here what is purely physical, there what is biological, and there what is spiritual. Physical interpretation, in so far as we adhere to it, is applicable to the whole of our perceived experience. But so is biological interpretation, and so . . . is psychological interpretation. At each level of interpretation the whole of our experience is covered.'[1]

5·3. This substitution of different levels for juxtaposed patches is the business primarily of the philosophy of Nature, but the more concrete a special science is the more are its students compelled in working at their own level to recognize it. 'Life', as Haldane remarks, 'becomes meaningless if

[1] *Philosophy of a Biologist*, p. 78; a book to which these sections owe much.

we regard it as other than an active struggle within an otherwise unco-ordinated chaos; and the more clearly we recognise how our universe appears apart from life, the more clearly does life appear to us.'[1] In making the substitution we must not forget that each level presupposes, and is the effort to constitute itself out of and over against, the level below it. Nevertheless, let us repeat, this does not mean that the lower level, or pieces of it, are miraculously transformed into the higher; that bread and water, e.g., are, to begin with, entities alien *in se* to the animal, and are then quite unintelligibly transubstantiated through digestion. It means that *for* the living organism its environment, even *qua* an opposed element confronting it, is not simply juxtaposed to it: its environment is not sheerly external to the organism, but an externality *within* it because *for* it. Life *is* a process of self-constitution and self-maintenance, and the *whole* environing world enters this process as an integral factor: the environment, even so far as it is hostile, is a constitutive moment in the definition of life, and not an alien patch contingently juxtaposed.

This problem of levels is, as I have said, primarily a philosophic problem. Natural science differs from philosophy because it must treat its world as independent of consciousness and innocent of values, and because it abstracts at each level from the level above it.[2] But no natural science can wholly ignore the relation of its own level to the level which lies beneath it.

5·4. The most obvious difficulty in this substitution of levels for juxtaposed patches lies, I think, in our tendency to presuppose space and time as a constant framework within which either relation—juxtaposition or difference of level— holds good: to express these very relations we can only find spatial metaphors. Yet space can belong only to a purely physical level, and if we are to hold that any level is temporal without being also spatial, then time must be taken as

---

[1] *Philosophy of a Biologist*, p. 91.
[2] Yet biology, if it is admitted to be teleological, is not wholly unconcerned with value in the sense of goodness. And any professedly empirical psychology is in the ambiguous position of offering to treat mind as an observable object independent of mind.

different in character at that level from what it is at a spatio-temporal level. This must be so if at each level the whole universe is in principle manifest.

Aristotle is half aware that the relation of animate to in-animate Nature, and of percipient to object, can only be solved if we take them as belonging respectively to mutually exclusive levels, and if we treat the higher level as self-con-stitutive against, but also out of, the level below it. So much is clearly implicit in his conception of the perceptive act as a single actualization of two potentialities. And when he treats this actualization as (*a*) on the part of the object a process of change, but (*b*) on the part of the percipient a timeless passage from potency to activity, he is, I think, con-scious that the change of level entails a change of temporal aspect. Nevertheless he often appears to lapse towards re-garding all the elements in the situation—organ, medium, perceptible thing, process, and timeless passage to activity—as being all together on one level.

6. If we now return from this digression and look again at the stages of Aristotle's *Scala Naturae*, we find that the connexion between actuality and activity, to which we con-cluded in Chapter II, § 6·1, is amply confirmed. The reci-procal transformation of the four elements, whose nature is scarcely more than a capacity of being moved; the instru-mentality of organic structures; the even tenor of self-maintenance and propagation which belongs to plant life; the intermittent nisus of sensory appetition in the brute; the will of man, whose higher spiritual life we have yet to con-sider—here is a scale on which passivity lessens from stage to stage. The changing thing at each stage is more nearly self-changing, though never wholly free. But it will repay us now to concentrate our attention particularly upon the imperfection, and the consequently defective intelligibility, of the lower stages of the scale.

6·1. If we apply causal analysis, we find that at these lower levels formal, final, and efficient causes tend to fall apart; form suffers extreme diremption, and matter is corre-spondingly prevalent. The four elements in their cyclical transformation do exist in order to subserve higher forms in the sublunary world; but also there is an order of fineness in them, and each does in transforming itself 'strive' to attain the higher elemental form above it. Moreover the formation of chemical compounds, with which the development of higher sublunary form begins, occurs only when transformation *breaks down*, and transformation always stops short of the fifth element, the yet finer ether of the spheres. The conspicuous aspect of causation here is always a comparatively external efficient cause, and so far as final cause is present it appears to split into two. Thus primarily the revolving spheres constitute an efficient cause of elemental transformation, but Aristotle sees in the cyclic character of this transformation a sort of self-assimilation to rotary movement; so that the four elements appear to seek two different ends, rotary movement and higher self-information in the more complex phases of the sublunary world. Whereas in the act of sense-perception two not quite homogeneous matters combine to subserve one form, here one matter seems to subserve two forms.

6.2. Thus everywhere the base of Aristotle's teleological structure reveals gaps and fissures. There is no need to linger over the detail of an obsolete cosmology, for Aristotle's firm rejection of external teleology—resuscitated by Christian piety in the shape of a Providence domesticated to the detail of daily life[1]—tells the same story in more modern guise. Though the crops perish in a drought, yet it does not rain in order that they may grow. Rain is a necessary condition of their growth, but it is not an intelligibly operating cause, because it contributes to a perfection which is not its own. Hence the other aspect, or moment, of this unfree necessity is contingency;[2] the relation of the two processes at any rate seems due to chance.

6.21. Aristotle, it is true, holds the only true cause to be form, either as Nature or as reason, and he maintains that

---

[1] Cf. Goethe's epigram:

> Welche Verehrung verdient der Weltenschöpfer, der gnädig,
> Als er den Korkbaum schuf, gleich auch die Stöpsel erfand.

> Glory to God Almighty who design'd
> The cork-tree for us, having corks in mind.

[2] The contingent, according to Aristotle, is what can be otherwise than as it is, and at most observes only a general rule in its behaviour.

chance as a cause is always posterior to them. That seems to imply that chance is just a word we use to cloak our ignorance. But he does sometimes incline towards accepting some real indeterminacy in things, particularly in order to afford scope for the exercise of human will, which in his *Ethics* he treats as operative in the sphere of the contingent and as therefore partially contingent in its results. In conduct, for example, the subject develops his own plastic emotional nature, and the development may go well or ill. Aristotle is far from the puerile error of equating freedom with contingency, but he recognizes that as freedom increases the attendant risk of caprice (contingency at the level of consciousness) grows *pari passu*. And again, in conduct as in Nature contingency and unfree—compulsive—necessity are inseparable aspects, or moments, of the same process. As any man who has at all reflected on his vices is perfectly well aware, capricious self-expression in the fulfilment of impulse is equally and at the same time a yielding to impulse.

6.3. Thus the ambiguity of matter forces itself on our attention for the third time. We have seen that matter, which is *per se* sheerly negative, yet presents itself as a positive complement of otherwise abstract form. We have found that to cause, which is *per se* form, a fourth, material moment is indispensable. The puzzle has now reappeared in the potentiality which in the process of its actualization is at once necessary and contingent.

IV

ARISTOTLE: NATURE AND
NATURAL SCIENCE

1. It is worth while, before we ascend beyond the natural world, to ask what sort of intelligible structure Nature on Aristotle's account presents.

The several stages of the scale which we have passed in review are distinct genera. Each relates to the one above it so that any one term of the series is to the next as that is to the proximately higher term; each presupposes and is a further development of its predecessor's nature. On the other hand, these genera are not coextensive. It is true that there are no tissues and organs save those which are combined in complex organic bodies, and no organic bodies save those which are actually animate as plants or animals. And it is true that every living tissue is some definite compound of the four elements. But (a) the analogical relation of genera does not in every case depend on the physical presence of the lower concrete in the higher. A plant contains chemical compounds as constituents, but an animal is not constituted of vegetables.[1] (b) Not every thing which belongs to one genus is also proximate matter within a more highly informed concrete. There are numerous compounds of the four elements besides those which combine to form tissue, and there are masses of earth, water, air, and fire which do not combine to form any sort of chemical compound.

1.1. Thus the structure of Nature, if we regard it as a hierarchy of genera, is pyramidal. As we examine it from base to summit we seem to find at each stage a number of points where development has been arrested; specific groups which display a peculiar character indifferent to higher information,[2] although this specific character still is a differentiation of a genus, and is itself, as we shall see, a term in a

[1] The transcendence in digestion of vegetable food is a comparatively unimportant exception.

[2] 'Higher' is, of course, here used in the sense opposite to that in which common formal logic applies the term to the wider and more comprehensive generic character.

developing series. The genus is thus connected on the one hand with other genera, on the other with its own internal specific variation; but generic and specific differentiation fail, it seems, together to constitute the clearly intelligible development of a single theme. Nature resists interpretation as a fully articulate system.

1·2. Accordingly Aristotle assigns to each genus a special demonstrative science, which he forbids to reason beyond the borders of its own province. The genus in relation to its species is to be regarded as a matter or potentiality which is actualized through a series of differentiae in and as a group of *infimae species*; only in its species is it real and intelligible. Only the *infima species* is strictly definable.

2. Species, then, *is* a term in a developing series of which the stages are stages of specification from genus to the final integration of genus in *infima species*. On the other hand, the several species do not, on what may be called Aristotle's official view, relate to one another as terms of a developing series, but are co-ordinate.[1]

2·1. The *infima species* thus appears to be, at any rate for the special scientist, the one fully real and intelligible entity of the world of Nature. The *infima species* is 'substance', Aristotle's name for what is fully real in its own right, that which has no contrary and admits of no degree.[2] Moreover, though it is the business of the metaphysician to consider the relation of genera to one another, it seems to be Aristotle's official view that no conclusions to which the metaphysician may come can in any way modify the truth of that direct immediate insight into the substantial nature of the *infimae species* which the trained special scientist possesses. In his intuitive grasp of the specific natures, the definable essences which are actualizations of the genus in specific differentiae, the special scientist can rest undisturbed by philosophic criticism, and also in the conclusions for which this insight provides him with premises.

3. Aristotle's account of the demonstrative reasoning in a special science is roughly as follows. The man of science

---

[1] i.e. at each level of differentiation between the genus and the *infimae species* lies a set of co-ordinate terms.

[2] e.g. man has no contrary and there are no degrees of manhood.

who is master of his subject has direct insight not only into these specific essences, these substantial natures which exist in their own right; he has also an immediate, intuitive grasp of (i) certain axioms, and (ii) certain 'essential accidents'. These terms require some explanation. (i) The axioms are the laws of contradiction and excluded middle, and certain other more special axioms. Axioms, at least in the case of the subsequently so-called laws of thought, are not premisses of demonstration but regulative canòns presupposed in scientific as in all other reasoning. On the other hand, the laws of contradiction and excluded middle are laws of thought only because they are, primarily, attributes of Being as such, essential characters of whatever *is*. (ii) The significance of the 'essential accidents' which figure among the elements of a special science can best be explained if we remember that matter is present everywhere in Nature, and in a degree which increases as we descend the *Scala Naturae*.[1] Since there is no sheer matter except primary matter, the increased prevalence of matter means that if a concrete thing belonging to a low level be analysed into matter and form, there must emerge a residue of form-determinations which does not enter into, is not integral to, the form which is taken as the essential form of the concrete thing, nor to its proximate matter; yet it does somehow belong to the thing. This residue, relatively to the essential form and its proximate matter, may be regarded as *mere* matter; *qua* a set of determinations, i.e., it is accidental in the sense of contingent and simply incidental to the thing. But between (*a*) these sheerly accidental characters which appear and vanish in the specimens quite contingently so far as the essential form is concerned, and (*b*) the substantial characters which are integral to the essential form, there are certain 'essential accidents' which do make a contribution to the essential development of the concrete thing. For in the realm which natural science studies the substantial *infimae species* are manifested to us as multiplicities of perceptible singular things which are concretes of matter and form. And though these singular things are in constant change, yet they change according to necessary laws which it is the business of the man of science to

---

[1] See ch. iii, § 6·1 above.

elicit. Hence the substantial *infimae species* are called by
Aristotle 'materiate forms', and he recognizes these properties of regular change, manifest in the singular things, as
essential, although he regards them as at the same time
'accidental' in the sense that they do not belong to the
elements which constitute and define the substantial specific
nature, viz. its genus and differentia. They are 'accidents'[1]
because they do not exist in their own right (substantially),
but only in dependence upon substance. He treats them as
'due to matter'.[2] But they are essential because they attach in
a degree to any and every specimen of the species, and because
the direct cause of their dependence on substance is one
element in the substantial nature of the species to which they
belong, one phase, that is to say, in the developing series of
logical actualization from genus to *infima species*.

There are also further essential accidents, properties whose
inherence in the species is more remote; i.e. the *proximate*
cause of their inherence is itself an essential accident.

3·1. Thus demonstration in a special science will be a
sorites of syllogisms. In the first, or basic, syllogism the
minor premiss will select some element within the specific
essence (normally, i.e. ideally, the differentia) and predicate
it of the species (the minor term); the major premiss will
predicate an essential accident, a property, of the specific
element, which thus becomes the middle term of the syllogism; the conclusion is accordingly a demonstration that a
property inheres in the species through and in virtue of one
selected element in the species. In the episyllogism the
property just proved to inhere in the species now becomes
the middle term, and through it the inherence—thus doubly
mediated—of a second property is demonstrated.[3]

3·11. This scheme of a special science as a body of conclusions demonstrated in chains of consequences which flow,
rigidly necessitated, from self-evident intuited premisses,
represents for Aristotle the ideal of a completed natural
science, not the method of discovery in science. He adapts it
from mathematics, in particular from geometry, without fully

---

[1] συμβεβηκότα.
[2] *Sc.* to proximate matter.
[3] The middle term thus in each case reflects the real cause of the inherence.

recognizing the difficulty of treating causal connexion in Nature entirely in terms of the inherence of attribute in substance. He conceives, however, that in mathematics certain general properties of all natural bodies, viz. numerability and the types of geometrical figuration, are abstracted and then treated as *quasi*-substances—number, triangle, &c. —in which the inherence of further properties can then be demonstrated. Though, historically speaking, he is adapting mathematical method to natural science, he regards the mathematical application of it, and not its use in natural science, as secondary. He will have nothing to do with the Pythagorean and Platonic view that numbers and figures are substantial.

4. The peg upon which his theory of scientific demonstration hangs is Aristotle's notion of the *infima species* as substance. This notion is the result of a compromise for which matter is again responsible.

4·1. To common sense it seems obvious that neither the abstract genera of Nature, nor the *infimae species* in which they are articulate and actual, are fully real and substantial. Rather it is the singular individual specimen of the natural species which in the world of Nature appears to exist in its own right. For what is real must be individual, and surely the singular specimen, the concrete of matter and form, is individual.

In the *Categories* Aristotle accepts this common-sense view, and it runs as an undercurrent, never wholly relinquished, through all his writings on Nature. He was never tempted to regard the abstract genus as fully real and substantial, and at one time it seemed to him quite logical to say that the genus, in itself a mere logical matter or potentiality, reaches final actualization and substantiality not in the species but only in the singular specimen.

4·2. But in *Metaphysics Z* Aristotle rejects this conclusion, and indeed the objections to it are strong and obvious. The singulars below specific differentiation are an indefinite multiplicity of concretes. Each is perhaps unique, but unique only *qua* this or that passing shape which cannot long sustain its being in 'the vast revolution of living and dying'. Form is the sole intelligible element in them, and form does nothing to explain their unique singularity. The uniqueness of each is no more than a complementary moment of the unintelligible endless multiplicity in which they come to be and perish, and Aristotle holds the principle—'alogical principle' perhaps—of such unintelligible diversity to be matter.

Moreover the singular as such is the object of sense-perception and not of thought, and singular uniqueness does not belong to the perceived thing apart from its being perceived. Sensible singularity is the character of being 'this', and it belongs to the content of the single actualization of *perceptum* and percipient. The unperceived perceptible, ambiguous though it be,[1] is neither the crude 'thing' of common sense nor a modern *sensum*.

4·21. When Aristotle wishes to speak of a singular, he never calls it a 'one' but very often a 'this'. Moreover 'this' implies 'that' and 'the other' and so on; i.e. the rudimentary universal, the attachment of 'this' to a vague multiplicity, is already present in any (human) awareness of 'this'. So much is implied in the fact that in the perceptive act form without matter is perceived, and Aristotle puts this by saying: 'Even if sense-perception as a faculty is of "the such" and not merely of a designable "this", yet one must at any rate actually perceive a designable "this", and at a definite present place and time.'[2] The definite quantitative character of being one of a plurality, on the other hand, involves *sensus communis* in its unspecialized and superior function of perceiving number. *A fortiori* number is not a character of the thing taken apart from sense-perception.

On the other hand, it must not be forgotten that on the view of substance which Aristotle maintains in the *Categories*, not any designable 'this' is substance, but only that which owes its unity to Nature, only the specimen of a species. For example, no casual fragment of earth, water, air, or fire would be a substance; nor, again, at the level of chemical composition any fragment of a mineral. Only the four totalities of the elements, and the totalities of each specific mineral, could claim the title.

[1] See ch. iii, § 4·5 above.
[2] *Posterior Analytics*, i, 87ᵇ 28–30.

4·3. The perceptible singular, then, cannot be substance. As Plato had been well aware, the singular is just what science—mathematical science at any rate—finds unintelligible; the geometer does not demonstrate truth about the singular figure as such, and Aristotle was now proposing to adapt the procedure of natural science to that of mathematics. Thus it would seem that real substance must be universal as well as individual. This had been recognized in the Platonic theory of Forms, but Plato had not been able to distinguish clearly in respect of their claims to reality the genus and the *infima species*. To Aristotle it appeared that if the genus is universal but relatively unreal because abstract, and if the singular is individual but as such opaque to thought, then the *infima species* is the only surviving candidate for the title of substance in the natural world. That is at least concrete and individual as against the genus, and universal as against the singular.

4·4. But this substantiation of the *infima species* does not result in a satisfactory theory of demonstration. Between the *infima species* and the singular specimens stand the essential properties. They are universal and so far intelligible, and they inhere necessarily in the substantial species; but they do not enter into the essence, being explicitly excluded from the substantial nature of the species. Accordingly thought in its grasp of the *infima species* is timeless intuition, but in reasoning demonstratively to the inherence of properties it is a discursive movement, its object ambiguously suspended between a substantial specific form and a multiplicity of concrete singular specimens.

Thus specific essence and inhering properties, and correspondingly intuition and *discursus*, are far from happily related. To provide initial premisses for the chain of demonstration Aristotle has to allow that not only the essence but also the property, as yet floating only nominally defined, can be an object of immediate intuition. The conclusion is dependent absolutely on the premisses, but it is in no sense a development of the premisses. Yet if this is so, it is hard to see how the *soi-disant* inference can be anything but a new and totally unconnected act of intuition.

4·41. If we attempt to apply causal analysis to the syllogism, the result conflicts hopelessly with the notion of an isolatedly substantial specific essence. The specific essence is the formal cause of the inhering property: the latter can only be defined by reference to the former. But occasionally Aristotle calls the premisses of syllogism its material cause, in which case the conclusion ('syllogism' and 'conclusion' are synonyms for Aristotle) must be the final cause. But if so, the real and intelligible nature grasped in thought is the conclusion, i.e. not the bare specific essence, but the essence together with its intelligibly inhering property; and the premisses, essence and floating property, are a mere undeveloped stage of this reality. We should in fact have to say that in the premisses the essence merely floats, like the property; it is not the plane figure bounded by three straight lines that we really *know* as a substantial reality, nor a creature barely defined as rational animal, but the triangle concrete in its properties and man in the concrete world of his activities.

4·5. So it becomes evident that although in Aristotle's eyes the premisses and conclusions of an ideally demonstrated special science would be strictly true and exempt from metaphysical criticism, yet this ideal contains after all an ineradicable defect. It cannot even in principle faithfully reflect the natural world.[1] When, despite his confidence in demonstration, Aristotle entitles the *infimae species* 'materiate forms' there is perhaps a hint that he recognizes this defect.

It is, however, far more important to notice that when Aristotle considers any subject-matter philosophically he invariably treats the 'species' (εἴδη) of it *not* as co-ordinate species of a genus but as falling into an order of development. He tacitly recognizes that mere co-ordination of specific differences is bare classification and no more, the potentiality of system but not its actual concrete articulation. When he

---

[1] As Aristotle clearly intends that it should. To him substance and accident are different kinds of Being (cf. ch. vi, § 4·1 below), and he regards the discursive movement of demonstration not as being, in contrast with rational intuition, the relative failure of the thinking subject to coincide with its object, but as perfectly reflecting the dependence of accident upon substance.

philosophizes he abandons the view that difference of kind excludes difference of degree, and treats each term after the first as a further modification and development of its predecessor. So each grade of 'soul' presupposes and is a further development of the grade below it, and each grade of 'soul' in effect itself subdivides into a graded series of functions, not into a bundle of merely co-ordinate faculties;[1] so in his moral philosophy Aristotle orders hierarchically the types of friendship and of political constitution, and also, I think, of justice; so in *De Anima*, 414[b] 28 ff., even the figures of plane geometry are said to fall into developing series. Aristotle's whole underlying conception of the mineral, vegetable, and animal kingdoms is quite obviously throughout hierarchical; he makes no pretence in philosophical practice of confining the analogical relation to the linkage of genus to genus. He leaves us in no doubt that philosophical insight is everywhere baffled until it can make of its object a scale of forms approximating to a highest form, a scale analogous in structure to the *Scala Universi* which embraces them all.[2]

Yet although he may tacitly recognize it, he never openly draws the obvious corollary that so far as thought presents to itself any subject-matter as no more than a genus of co-ordinate species, so far it has failed to comprehend it as more than a unity of bare differences; so far it has grasped the fact and not the reasoned fact.

4·51. We may add that Aristotle commonly regards the accidental property[3] as a *quasi*-genus which is specified through its variations of degree. The logical structure of this *quasi*-genus is thus markedly different from that of a genus of substantial *infimae species*. It is constituted of two contrary opposites, one of which is the more actual, the other the more potential or privative. The contraries blend in various proportions to differentiate a graded series of species. Colours, for example, mingle white and black to constitute the series of specific colours. The structure of such a

---

[1] In ch. iii, § 4·7, we had an instance of this.

[2] The most striking passage in which Aristotle attempts to express the *Scala Universi* as he sees it is *Metaphysics*, 1075[a] 11–25 (cited in my *Aristotle*, pp. 172–3).

[3] See § 3 above.

quasi-genus is thus far closer to the hierarchical nature which any philosophical subject-matter presents than to Aristotle's official genus.

5. From every point of view the Aristotelian system of Nature has shown itself obfuscated with matter and riddled with contingency, and we have not found its author always in one mind. We have now to glance at the higher stages of the *Scala Universi*. We have already seen something of human practical activity, and in discussing natural science we have presupposed thought, making an anticipatory use of the products of human theorizing. We must now make good this anticipation and see how thought develops from sense-perception, and we must examine the claim of the *infima species*, rational animal, to be sole occupant of the highest natural stage of the scale, and yet to transcend Nature in thought as it transcends Nature in action.

V

ARISTOTLE: SENSE AND THOUGHT

1. THE act of sense-perception is a single actualization, though not without residue, of two potentials. The perceptible stimulates this concrete act of awareness, yet in the act it is at least in part itself fulfilled; it actualizes its own nature. But sense-perception is a phase in a developing series of information. In man, even in most brutes, the content of the perceptual act persists as what, for want of a better word, may be called an 'image'.[1] But this 'persistence' is development, and even physiologically considered the 'image' is not a static imprint but a process.

In this image, though it is still highly material and potential, the germ of universality present in the act of sense-perception has become more explicit and actualized, and it is vital for our subsequent understanding of Hegel to pay close attention here to Aristotle's doctrine and its implications.

2. In imagination, then, a function closely connected by Aristotle with *sensus communis* and also with memory, the content of sense-perception is developed, although the development is not very much more than a persistence. If the single actualization at this level be analysed into two potential factors, imagining subject and imagined object, these factors will no longer be two 'physical' things: imagination has no organ of its own other than the heart, and no 'imaginable' actualizes with it other than the perceptible of the stage below. That is to say, there is not at this stage a fresh act of communication with an 'outer' world. By imagination the subject becomes aware of what he had perceived as in fact a persistent, as something after all more than a mere fugitive *perceptum*; but he does not in imagination make a fresh contact. Correspondingly, to become an image is a further development of the original *perceptum*'s own nature, and this development takes place within the content of the subject's activity. When imagination develops into thought, there is again no fresh contact with an 'external' world.

On the other hand, just as the single act of sense-percep-

[1] The German *Vorstellung* renders Aristotle's φάντασμα fairly correctly.

tion was not without residue—we had to presuppose a perceptible and an organ existing in some sort of potential state apart from actual perception—so imagination fails to absorb wholly the sense-perception of which it is the higher development. We do 'image', and still at the same time perceive; or, to put it less crudely, we have never in 'imaging' wholly passed beyond perceiving.

2·1. Nevertheless Aristotle's doctrine justifies no realist conception of the natural world as possessing its character in independence of, and indifference to, mind. Nature is even more than the essential *correlate* of a highly developed form of mind: it is something which is only actual as the *object and content* of mind. Nature and mind are not merely concurrent in their development: their single actualization has its seat in mind.

Aristotle is, of course, not in full possession of this thought. Some of the shortcomings in his theory we have already observed,[1] and we shall find others. Yet if we take—as we must—the causal analysis as guiding thread, we cannot escape the inference that the formal cause of Nature is mind.

2·2. It may be objected by common sense that if the real nature of the object be actualized only in and as the subject's activity, we have nothing but the mysterious residue of the unperceived perceptible between us and an absurd theory that the object achieves its real nature indifferently in any one of a number of separate and casual perceptive acts performed by a conscious subject—or, indeed, by a multiplicity of conscious subjects.

The answer is, I believe, at least implicit in Aristotle's teaching, though it cannot be said to have become explicit in philosophy before Kant formulated his doctrine of the transcendental unity of apperception—if even then. If we bear this in mind, it may be fairly put as follows. The distinctive content of sense-perception is at once a 'this' and a 'such', both a singular and a rudimentary universal.[2] But in that content the subject is actualized in one with its object. Aristotle himself holds that we are in sense-perception self-conscious.[3] He appears, it is true, to be thinking of

---

[1] Cf. ch. iii, §§ 4·5 and 4·8 above.   [2] Cf. ch. iv, § 4·21 above.
[3] Cf. ch. iii, § 4·7.

a relatively incidental self-distinction of the subject from its object, yet on his own account of the perceptive act the one content is the actualized subject as well as the actualized object. If so, the 'this' is equally and also this momentarily active 'I', and the 'such' is equally and also a *universal* subject. Hence the perceptive function of a conscious subject is not a casual multiplicity of separate acts, and the privacy of the percipient's function is less inviolable than common sense is apt to suppose. The *whole* world of possible total *perceptum*, and a correlative *universal* subject capable in principle of perceiving it, are implied and operative in any supposedly separate and private act of sense-perception. In explicitly perceiving 'this' and (incidentally) myself, I implicitly perceive 'this-such', and recognize it as 'this-such' for *any* percipient. For 'this' clearly implies more than 'this-for-me'; it is 'deictic', and to point is to assume the identity of other percipients with oneself. Indeed, if this were not so, sense-perception could never develop into imagination and thought. For the universality of the subject becomes more explicit in imagination and still more explicit in thought; and clearly this development is only possible if the subject of sense-perception is already *in posse* universal. The other condition of its possibility is that on each level of conscious function there is some imperfection: the union of subject and object is not complete, and function at the higher level can never quite dispense with function at the lower.[1]

3. If now, ignoring the elaboration of imagination in memory and recollection, we carry forward this development to thought, we shall find Aristotle remarkably—perhaps unduly—indifferent to that separateness of one conscious subject from another which seems so obvious to common sense. But Aristotle was not unaware that familiarity breeds ignorance as often as contempt.

The highest human level to which the single actualization of subject and object reaches is reason (νοῦς). Aristotle's doctrine of νοῦς is notoriously difficult, and any short account of it must run the risk of being a mere dogmatical cutting of the knots.

3·1. Reason, so far passive, is stimulated by the 'image',

[1] Cf. § 2 above.

and receives from it a form which is *per se* intelligible, a universal developed far beyond the mere form without matter which the act of sense-perception absorbs. This form is in fact the essence of the object, the substantial specific form which we discussed in Chapter IV. But reason in man knows this form only in—not as but in—the 'image'. The form is so far a materiate form, and it would seem that thought can no more dispense with imagination than imagination could dispense with sense-perception. On the other hand, when reason is thus stimulated to actual knowledge, the single actualization of subject and object *is* a union without residue, unreservedly complete: fully actual knowledge is utterly identical with what is known, and in this knowing reason knows itself. Moreover, the form which has been operative in man without a break from sense-perception upward now becomes explicit in the activity which constitutes man's essential nature. Man is rational, and the efficient cause—indeed the final and formal cause too—which actualizes passive reason[1] is not the mere stimulating 'image' but an essentially active reason.

3·2. Here begins the difficulty. For Aristotle seems in danger of severing active reason altogether from human nature, although that is not his intention. The actualization of passive by active reason does not readily submit to a deeper application of the causal analysis. Unlike sense, which when inactive still possesses an organ and therefore has still some character of its own, passive reason, or reason in its passive moment, must be totally devoid of any character. It is, says Aristotle, unmixed with the body, and it uses no organ; and it shares no character with anything potentially its object.[2] If it did, this would be bound to intrude and prevent perfect identity in actualization with the object; i.e. in the object of complete knowledge there is no residual character which it possesses apart from being known.

3·3. The relation of passive to active reason is most obscure. Aristotle may possibly mean that the image is

---

[1] One should perhaps say 'reason *qua* passive', but just here lies the problem, as the next section will show.

[2] i.e. there is nothing analogous to the rough generic identity shared by organ and perceptible.

instrumental to reason only in the knowing of materiate forms and in the discursive movement of thought from these to the properties which inhere in them, such knowing not being fully actual knowing.[1] But even if this interpretation, neither everywhere supported by Aristotle's language nor easily reconciled with his apparent exemption of the specific form from metaphysical criticism, be correct, nevertheless a chasm then occurs between the reason which knows the materiate form and that perfect union of subject and object in active reason, in which self-consciousness is no longer a by-product but the essence of the union. In *De Anima*, 408ᵇ 25 ff., reason[2] is said to be immortal and eternal, whereas discursive thinking (διάνοια), love, hate, and memory are functions, 'not of the reason but of that which has reason, in so far as it has it', and they perish at death. Here the impression given is that reason is something alien, temporarily, even casually, lodged in a man. Moreover, since διάνοια is the only intellectual activity explicitly condemned to mortality, intuition of the specific materiate form would seem to be an integral element of the eternal, impersonal, reason from which death divides us, and the impassable gulf between intuitive and discursive thought of the world of Nature, which we observed in Chapter IV, § 4·4, appears to be confirmed.

And yet it is also said by Aristotle that reason (and he must in the context[3] mean active reason) 'would seem to be each man himself'.

4. I have dwelt on this apparent self-contradiction in Aristotle, because the whole problem which arose with the notion of matter and form begins here to come to a head. Aristotle is quite clear that only the universal no longer abstract nor owing anything to matter but concretely individual can be truly known; that true knowledge is therefore a *timeless* immediate intuition without *discursus*; that

---

[1] This seems to be confirmed by a passage in which he says that we know a specific essence by something different from sense, 'either wholly separate from sense or related to it as a line bent back is to the same line straightened' (*De Anima*, 429ᵇ 16). The suggestion is that reason works reflectively, developing and perfecting its lower sensuous self.

[2] No distinction is here drawn between active and passive reason.

[3] *Nicomachean Ethics*, 1177ᵇ 30–78ᵃ 7.

such a knowing is the identity of mind with its object, i.e. is essentially and not incidentally self-consciousness. He is further clear that such a knowing cannot possibly be adjectival to a subject which is individual in the sense of being a singular subject among an indefinite plurality of other such individual subjects. If truth is universal, although in its highest form also individual, then neither can it be the truth of singular things as such, nor can it be the possession of a singular subject as such. A man in the very act of judging a proposition true, is claiming that its truth is independent of his act *qua* the act of a singular judging subject. The content of his judgement, so far as it is merely *his*, is merely his opinion.[1]

4·1. I have little doubt that the implication of Aristotle's teaching is that the individual subject of experience (in the sense of a singular subject maintaining himself distinct from other experient subjects) originates in sense-perception, develops through practical activity, which Aristotle rates lower than theoretical, and ceases to be thus distinct in at any rate the highest phase of theoretical thinking. Moreover, this individual subject, in those phases of his development which do entail this self-distinction, does yet not maintain himself as an isolated atom.[2] No absolutely isolated atom can be, be experienced, or experience itself.[3] And in development beyond sense-perception—in practice, e.g.—this distinctness of the subject only grows *pari passu*, though often in conflict, with a universal nature which it shares with other subjects of experience. Hence, the logic which assigns to this development a culmination in which all mere separation and privacy of individuals will have vanished, appears irresistible.[4] And if this culmination be a true knowing, any theory of truth that is not purely Protagorean seems forced to accept it.

[1] It is obvious that a man's perceivings and imaginings are private to himself as his thoughts are not. Their comparative incommunicability is common enough matter of experience.

[2] That at the level of sense-perception this is so we saw in § 2·2 above.

[3] The very phrase 'isolated atom' enters discourse only in virtue of a relative meaning conferred upon it within a limited sphere of relevance.

[4] The argument here assumes with Aristotle (and also Hegel) that the highest form of spiritual experience is *par excellence* theoretical.

4·2. Yet this conclusion is open to strong objection. It may seem plausible so long as we take mathematics, and even natural science, as typical of true knowing. To mathematical truth the individual humanity of the mathematician does seem to be merely irrelevant. But (*a*) if this is so, and if mathematics is a typical product of man's highest cognitive powers, then man's theoretical activity must be something quite apart from the rest of his nature, from, for example, his practical activity. Theory and practice on this account do not merely bifurcate; they do not exhibit any common root. And (*b*) this is not Aristotle's view. He holds that man in his highest cognitive activity (which mathematical and scientific demonstration, if it be disconnected from philosophical thought, does *not* typify)[1] fulfils his *whole* nature. It is true that Aristotle breaks with Plato so far as to deny that metaphysical insight into the ultimately real is the essential condition of moral action, and to that extent implies a bifurcation of spiritual power; but he does clearly hold that practical wisdom is a presupposition of metaphysical insight. For metaphysical insight is, on his view, insight into the real and the good as one. Hence, if reason is the culmination which man's whole spiritual development postulates as its formal cause, it must be shown to be a culmination something more than formally relevant to human aspiration. But if reason is perfect in itself and *causa sui*, it must tend to become utterly remote from the preceding stages of the scale.

4·3. In general, if within a hierarchical system which ascends in degrees of reality and perfection the final stage is fully real and perfect *in se*, can this final stage fail to be indifferent to the preceding stages, of whose relative reality and perfection it is nevertheless postulated to be the criterion? If it is *pure* form and actuality, can the preceding stages be its proximate *matter*? But if they are not, can it retain any connexion with them? And are we not in danger of an analogous break between every stage and its predecessors?

---

[1] The specific forms, mathematical and natural, though immediately intuited, are yet only known in images; see § 3·1 above.

VI

ARISTOTLE: GOD

1. THE summit of the *Scala Universi* is God. On the view of some great Aristotelians active reason is God. If it is, we must say that man in his flashes of the highest metaphysical insight so knows God as to be *eo ipso* identical with God, whose nature is said by Aristotle to be νόησις νοήσεως, a timeless activity of thought with itself as object; an absolute self-consciousness, i.e., in which the active self as subject knows and is identical with its actively knowing self.

More probably active reason is not God. Aristotle calls metaphysical thinking theology, but he does not confine divinity to God.[1] There are certain astral intelligences which move the star-bearing aetherial spheres, and they too are divine. He speaks in his *Ethics* of reason as either divine or only the most divine element in us, which suggests that active reason, and above it the astral intelligences, are stages intermediate between man and God.

But whatever be the precise connexion of active reason with God, the problem of its connexion with man now reappears as the problem of God's relation to the world. In the two following Sections this is expressed in the shape of an antinomy.

2. God is immanent in the world. For God is the ultimate formal cause of all things. He is the fully perfect actuality, and therefore the sole criterion by which the partially real stages of the *Scala Universi* can be defined and graded. As final cause God is the supreme Good, and the essential nature of all things is, according to the degree of their reality, a tendency, a nisus, or a conscious striving to assimilate themselves to the goodness of God, which is one with his intelligence. In philosophic man it may perhaps be even a self-identification. As efficient cause God moves the spheres and mediately all sublunary cyclical process; but this efficacy is not severed from his activity as final cause, for he moves as the object of love. Moreover, Aristotle

[1] Prof. J. A. Smith holds that Aristotle's 'theology' is the science of the divine, not of God or gods; see *Philosophy*, vol. x, no. 37, 1935.

distinguishes the respective functions of the metaphysician and the special scientist by assigning to the former Being as a whole for his province, to the latter some part of Being.

God, then, must surely be *forma informans*, immanent in the world of change.

3. God utterly transcends the world. He is 'a substance eternal, without motion, and separate from sensible things'.[1] As the world's form he is a *forma assistens*, not *informans*; for a *forma informans* informs a proximate matter, and pure form can have no matter. As perfect substance God is not an essence manifest in multiple singulars of which it is predicable. Between his existence and what he is there is no distinction. Neither a noun substantive nor an adjective suffices to express his nature. He is God, but that is to say he is good; he is good, but that is to say that he is God.[2] Moreover, as efficient cause of the world God moves, himself unmoved. He does not, like the moving body or the perceptible thing, realize his potentiality in that which he moves, because he is not process but pure activity wherein is no moment of potentiality. Again, God does not reciprocate the world's love; as final cause he is analogous rather to the serenely unconscious object of a passion which dominates and controls the life of an unconfessed lover. In true human love each is his lover's other self, but if man identifies himself with God, yet God does not identify himself with man. Further, the metaphysician studies Being as a whole because he studies not God only but also, in the light of God, the specific essences of Nature, which, too, are substances real in their station; and because he reflects on such general principles as matter and form, potential and actual, cause and effect. In fact, in most of his writings on Nature Aristotle speaks as a metaphysician, not as a special scientist. He works always in terms of the developing series whether he is discussing genera or what the special scientist would treat as co-ordinate species.[3]

---

[1] *Metaphysics*, 1073ª 4.

[2] For 'good' we may equally well here substitute 'real' and also 'intelligible', but we must remember that the fully real is the fully active, that the perfectly good is the fully active good, and that that which alone is perfectly intelligible is a perfect intelligence.   [3] Cf. ch. iv, § 4·5 above.

3·1. This separateness of God as *forma assistens* of the world is again confirmed when we examine more closely Aristotle's conception of pure activity. Activity, ἐνέργεια—to which, as we have seen, the form and actuality of each ascending phase of the scale approximates more nearly—is very sharply distinguished by Aristotle from process. *Mere* process would be absolutely contingent variation, below any distinction between transformation and alteration, the analogue of primary matter; pure activity is the complete characterization of pure form. Between them fall all shapes of change in the world. Each of these is a development up to, and a decline from, a climax of relative perfection. But in each of them this perfection, or consummation, is immanent in a different degree. In the almost sheerly transeunt causality of compulsory movement, for instance, the nature of the impelling body is realized indifferently in an indefinite series of impelled, and in their turn impelling, bodies. The process is hardly development at all. Growth is development, and the end is immanent in the adult; but it is only partially immanent in the stages before and after maturity. Art constitutes, as it were, a side-step and a fresh start. Man begins to react upon Nature, whose product he is. In art the consummation lies outside the process leading to it, consisting as it does in the finished artefact. Only if the product is good is the artist called a good artist. In conduct the end, or consummation, is still distinguishable from the process of effort towards its realization, but moral goodness in some measure resides in the effort itself; the end, that is to say, is in some measure immanent in the process which actualizes it. In short, in conduct the separation of climax from process begins to disappear, and it becomes clear that the types of temporal change are a developing series approximating to a timeless activity in which there is no distinction of process from climax. If this is to be described in temporal terminology, it must be called complete and perfect at any and every moment of itself. But such terminology is inappropriate; for time is the measure, the essential countable character, of change, and temporal process is a character only of the perceptible world. But such an activity—timelessly actual as God's nature and realized also, it would seem, in occasional flashes by man—is not an activity which realizes itself in the processes of the world. God moves, himself unmoved; he does not realize himself in and as the world he moves.

3·11. Again, God and the world are not related as Spinoza's *natura naturans* and *natura naturata*. In the world's dependence upon God there is something akin to the dependence of the inhering property, the essential accident, upon the *infima species* which is its cause. And the Spinozistic conception of substance and mode springs ultimately from Aristotle's doctrine of specific substance and essential accident. But despite these affinities we cannot interpret the Aristotelian world of change either as a complex of Spinozistic modes, or as a property, or complex of properties, inhering in God. The world of change has its own substances, and God has no accidents.

4. The balance of evidence indubitably points to a total severance of God from the world which he moves. Yet if Aristotle had whole-heartedly accepted such a position, he must, I think, have drawn the conclusion that, since pure activity is not process, it cannot move a world external to itself.[1] His God must have become at most the condition or occasion of movement in the cosmos, and not its cause. With that his whole position must have broken down, and this might have led him towards the view that pure activity must be at once self-containing and all-comprehensive. In actual fact he compromises. Although he regards pure activity as timeless, he cannot get quite beyond conceiving it as process in time. The notion of an unmoved mover— even if he move through love—is an unstable intermediate conception between process and activity, and it is a contradiction. Hence although one cannot doubt that on Aristotle's view the structural type which everywhere philosophic insight reveals is a hierarchy within which the ascending stages form a developing scale, yet the highest stage tends, against Aristotle's intention, to stand apart. In God the whole meaning of the world is to be found, but the perfection of God precludes the possibility of reciprocal relation between him

---

[1] And the analogous conclusion, too, that absolutely self-evident premisses cannot necessitate any conclusion; cf. ch. iv, § 4·4.

and the world, and Aristotle can find no alternative but a one-way relation: the world is related to God, but God is unrelated to the world. The perfect substance without accidents, which is pure form and pure activity, becomes self-enclosed in its essential perfection, a *forma assistens*, not a *forma informans*. Below God come substances which are somehow real in their own right, and yet the status of these lower realities is ambiguous. The special scientist can select and study a group of them, a set of specific forms in which a genus is actual; but he finds that certain accidental properties necessarily inhere in those specific forms, and that this inherence is a one-way relation something analogous to the one-way relation between the world and God. But to the philosopher these species—although their independent status apparently on Aristotle's view remains unimpaired—reveal their allegiance to the whole *Scala Universi*. They reveal it not only through their genus, which falls into place in the developing series of genera, but in the fact that in practice the philosopher can only treat them as themselves forming a hierarchy of more and less perfect phases. And when he does so, the highest stage of the hierarchy tends to sever itself from the stage below it, in imitation, as it were, of God's transcendence of the world.

4·1. The philosopher, moreover, cannot expel contingency from his vision of the universe. In the lower spheres of Nature contingency may perhaps be a cloak for ignorance, but the properties, accidental and due to matter, yet universal and inhering essentially, cannot be so dismissed. So much at least the schema of Aristotle's categories makes clear. For the ten categories, though a more or less empirical assemblage, are a product of philosophical thinking. They are one way in which the philosopher attempts to order the universe. And the categories express—one might almost say embalm—the distinction of substance and accident. The whole developing series of substances from God down to the four elements falls under substance, the first category; the remaining nine categories—*quantum, quale,* and the rest—represent in a rough order, which is neither a definite developing series nor a mere co-ordinate classification, all the heads under which accidents, essential or contingent, fall.

The categories are the puzzle of the Aristotelian system,[1] but at any rate they serve to show its failure to digest matter and contingency. The *Scala Universi* is a hierarchy of substances which in different degrees approximate to God, though substance does not in itself admit of differences of degree.[2] The nine accidental categories, on the other hand, constitute a rudimentary hierarchy within which accidents are ordered according to the varying degree of necessity and intimacy with which they inhere in substance, and accidents do in themselves admit difference of degree. These two systems both grade reality, or Being, as Aristotle calls it, and inasmuch as God is perfect substance they coincide at their summits. But elsewhere they are neither coincident nor congruent. When we learn, too, that there are certain other all-pervasive characters which, like Being, fall directly into genera and have a different sense in each category—not-being, unity and plurality (of which same and different, like and unlike, are subordinate types), good and evil—it becomes yet more evident that Aristotle's philosophy of matter and form, potential and actual, accident and substance, fails to elaborate itself into a single consistent system. Yet it still stands as the basis of European speculation.

5. To conclude this sketch of Aristotle's teaching and facilitate transition to Hegel, we may perhaps offer this clue to the relation between Aristotelianism and modern philosophy. We must, I think, select the threefold antithesis of matter and form, potential and actual, material and formal (final and efficient) cause, as expressing the distinctive Aristotelian principle.[3] This is not realism, for a consistent realist

---

[1] The categories are *summa genera*, not species, of Being. They ought therefore to constitute a developing series, but beyond asserting the priority of substance to the rest Aristotle nowhere states any principle on which they are to be ordered. Moreover, the difficulty discussed in ch. iv, §§ 4·4 and 4·41, is here obvious on a grand scale. Accident has a partial reality, which consists in its inherence in substance; but substance and accident are different *genera* of Being, and substance is real *per se*, in its own right. Hence accident cannot owe its whole nature to substance (it is not a degree of substance), and between them a chasm emerges analogous to the chasm between God and all lower substances.

[2] See ch. iv, § 2·1 above.

[3] Rather than substance and accident.

must reject unreservedly the distinction of being potentially from being actually. On the other hand, though it may be potentially, it is not actually, idealism. Intelligence crowns the Aristotelian *Scala Universi*, but sense-perception and thought remain special cases of the principle: Aristotle's account of them does not warrant an interpretation of his universe in terms of appearance and reality.

But it must be remembered that Hegel was the first 'modern' philosopher to make a deep and fruitful study of Aristotle's works.

VII

TRANSITION TO HEGEL

1. THAT philosophic insight must everywhere reveal a scale of development from less to greater perfection is the legacy bequeathed by the Hellenic thought which culminates in Aristotle. But Aristotle left what was at once a solution and a problem. We have seen the principle of development take shape in his system both as the temporal process of the growing and decaying singular, and also as a *Scala Universi* wherein the levels exhibit an order of developedness, but are not stages of a temporal process. In the relation of accident to substance the same thought finds expression in a different shape. But these various applications of one principle do not, we found, combine to express one perfectly coherent developing system. Contingency besets the lower levels, and a chasm severs the culminating stage from the stages which precede it.

2. It will be instructive, I think, to contrast Hegel's general philosophical position with Aristotle's as if Hegel had reached his own view simply through the effort to solve the problem as Aristotle left it. Of course he did not. He saw in every great philosopher a solution and a restatement of the whole problem of philosophy, and in his constructive works Kant's name recurs far oftener than Aristotle's. Yet in Hegel's posthumously published lectures on the History of Philosophy about three times as much space is devoted to Aristotle as to any later thinker, and about the same amount to Plato. There can be no doubt that, man for man, Hegel held 'the teachers of the human race', as he calls them, greater than any of their successors. Therefore, since we cannot set down the whole history of philosophy as an introduction to Hegel, a direct comparison of his thought with Aristotle's will perhaps falsify their true relation less than any other simplifying device.

2·1. Hegel, then let us say, accepted the general Aristotelian principle of development. He strove to close the chasm between the absolutely real and the relatively potential by recasting and absorbing within the absolutely real the whole succession of stages which in the Aristotelian system had led up to but failed to reach it; and he endeavoured in so doing to dominate the residue of contingency which Aristotle had abandoned as intractable.

2·2. For Hegel Aristotle's supreme achievement was his identification of fully substantial being with spirit (*Geist*), and his firmly grasped conception of spirit as in its essence activity; not, i.e., as that which has activity and is active, but as that which *is* activity. Plato, in Hegel's view, had not reached this conception. His Forms tend on the whole to remain ineffectively divorced from the world, and so far as that is so they are mere abstract universals.[1]

2·21. Moreover—and here in particular is Hegel's starting-point—Aristotle had defined this activity as the utter union of subject and object, the knowing which knows its knowing self;[2] and he had treated sense-perception as a union in the percipient subject of two actualizations, a union imperfect but prefiguring and approximating to the divine self-knowing. But he had shown no clear and necessary course of development from imperfect to perfect union of subject and object, and on the lower levels of Nature he had merely indicated a few rude analogues of it. Hegel, on the other hand, conceived the lower stages of the *Scala Naturae* as far more closely analogous to this union, which in fact he held to be the clue to the whole *Scala*. Hegel strove to unite the fully actual and the partly potential by bringing the lower levels of the *Scala* within the ambitus of an all-embracing correlativity of subject and object; to develop the distinction of potential and actual into that of apparent and real without giving to 'appearance' a subjectivist meaning.[3] When Aristotle analysed the partially developed as being at once potential and actual, his philosophic position was not realist. But equally it was not idealist:[4] Aristotle was still in some measure speaking the language of an external spectator.

---

[1] See, however, ch. x, § 2·1 below.

[2] On the whole Plato's Forms and the soul which knows them remain merely kindred and not identical.

[3] i.e. not intending the mere common-sense image-thought of a change on the part of an onlooker from obscure to clear vision of a thing which remains constant and indifferent to the change.

[4] Cf. ch. vi, § 5 above.

Hegel's method of reformulating the Aristotelian half-truth is to abandon the onlooker's attitude, and to seek the nature of the partially developed by asking first what it is *for itself*.[1] Then, if the subject of inquiry is self-conscious, it can be said actually to be so much as it is aware that it is, and to be only potentially so far as it fails to be fully aware what its own real nature is. Hegel further supposes that an analogous interpretation is possible when the subject of inquiry is not in the ordinary sense of the term self-conscious, and even when it is not conscious at all.[2]

3. Yet we must not lose wholly from sight the intervening influences which determined in general the course of Hegel's reconstruction, and in particular directed his attention upon Aristotle's theory of sense-perception and knowledge.

Scepticism was precluded by the *naïveté*, whether it be of youth or genius, which characterizes the Platonic and Aristotelian thought, and it was not permissible to medieval piety. In the Scholastic philosophy the realist-nominalist controversy had assumed a *de facto* correlation of mind and world. The problem was to decide what belonged to *ratio* and what to *res*, not the very validity of the distinction between them. Descartes was the first Christian to ponder the very possibility of knowing, and so to give a new prominence to the theory of knowledge. As students of Nature the Scholastics had disdained the discipline of observation and experiment, and achieved little but the corruption of Aristotle; but to them Nature had seemed at least not unakin to mind. Though their interest was in heaven rather than earth, the general Aristotelian notion of analogy between man and Nature had survived. On the other hand, the successful Cartesian analysis of Nature (including the living organism) in terms of extension and motion seemed to make of Nature something quite alien to mind. Descartes's dubitation had terminated upon the certainty of the self in any and every act of *cogitatio*, but his subsequent expansion of the *ego* into individual thinking substance had led to a doctrine of two starkly opposed substances sustained in commerce by God.

---

[1] For Hegel's view of the conditions of philosophic interpretation see ch. viii, §§ 3·2 ff. below.   [2] See ibid., §§ 4 ff.

4. But it soon became clear that this divine mediation is merely assumed. When Occasionalism had made the chasm obvious, Spinoza tried to mend it with a theory of God as the one all-comprising substance, but he could not absorb within God the philosophizing subject. Leibniz posited a multiplicity of all-representative monadic substances stated to culminate in God but in effect owing their order to a divine harmonizing which remains external to the system.

5. From these brilliant attempts to transform the notion of substance—especially from Spinozism—Hegel drew far more than can here be made apparent, but he saw in the Critical Philosophy a further indispensable step towards establishing the true relation of substance and subject. Kant had cast back to the Cartesian *ego*, exposed its pretensions to substantiality, and reinterpreted it as the transcendental unity of apperception. But his gigantic effort to combine the notion of the subject as the primary formal condition of a unitary objective world of experience with that of a matter deriving from perhaps the same, perhaps a different, source had left the situation unclear. For the Cartesian dualism of two substances Kant seemed to have substituted a twofold dualism: (*a*) between thought and sense, and (*b*) between the phenomenal world—the concrete within which, speaking roughly, thought and sense are related as form and matter—and the thing-in-itself. He had shown that subject is a higher (or deeper) notion than substance; he had clearly distinguished the transcendental *ego* from the empirical self, using to express the former the formula 'I = I', and treating it as the fundamental principle of all synthesis. But he had not seen that the mind's synthetic activity is an overreaching and inclusion of its object, an activity of self-consciousness wherein the object is not an external correlate but a constituent moment mediating what would otherwise remain the bare identity, the empty tautologous judgement, 'I = I'. He had not fully grasped that the 'original' unity of apperception, as he himself calls it, must be 'original' in the sense of being prior to the distinction of thought and being, and therefore not itself either merely subjective or merely objective. Instead he had (or so Hegel held) made of thought a mere subjective activity.

6. Fichte had come nearer to realizing this 'original' unity. It was Fichte's view that any man reflecting on what he means by calling himself 'I', must discover that he is thereby affirming himself; i.e. he must find that he is at the same time subject and object. This identity of subject and object in one indivisible free act is the very nature of the *ego*. Hence Fichte offers as the first fundamental proposition of his *Wissenschaftslehre*: The *ego* posits originally and simply its own being. This *ego* is of course not the singular individual self, but Kant's transcendental subject, and the bare formal expression of this first proposition is the law of identity. That is to say, 'A = A' expresses abstractly the first fundamental presupposition of all thought, viz. that no identity of object can be thought apart from the identity of the thinking subject.

6·1. Fichte's second fundamental proposition marks his advance upon Kant. Abstractly expressed, it is 'Not-A is not A'. Just as the *ego* of the first proposition is not the singular individual self, so this not-A is neither a particular object nor the Kantian thing-in-itself. The second proposition expresses the distinction of object from subject. This distinction the first proposition, which identifies subject and object, must imply as no less 'original' than itself, no less fundamentally presupposed in all further movement of thought, which is always in a broad sense self-consciousness.

6·2. But each of these propositions renders the other self-contradictory: to posit this *non-ego* is to negate the *ego*, but the *non-ego* is only posited at all *through* the *ego*. Fichte, accepting Spinoza's view that to negate is to determine in the sense of to limit, solves the contradiction with a third fundamental proposition which synthesizes the thesis and antithesis wherein the first and second propositions respectively consist: Since the *ego* both posits and negates itself, it must posit itself as a determinable (i.e. limitable) *ego* limited by a correspondingly determinable *non-ego*, and reciprocally determining (i.e. limiting) that *non-ego*.

6·3. This third proposition, as synthesizing the other two, thus turns out to be the complete expression of the 'original' presupposition, the minimal character of *any* rational activity. But it breaks again into two opposed propositions. For it evidently signifies that the *ego* posits (A) itself as determined by the *non-ego*, and (B) the *non-ego* as determined by itself, the *ego*. (A) is the starting-point of theoretical activity, and the fundamental proposition of theoretical *Wissenschaftslehre*; (B) is the starting-point of practical activity, and the fundamental proposition of practical *Wissenschaftslehre*. The business of theoretical *Wissenschaftslehre* is to develop both the logical categories involved in the progressive recognition of the *non-ego* by the *ego*, and also the modes in which cognitive intelligence progressively manifests itself; i.e. to complete the two tasks begun in Kant's objective and subjective deductions of the categories respectively. But Fichte, like Kant, regarded both categories and modes of cognitive intelligence as in themselves purely formal. 'It was', says Robert Adamson,[1] 'for him a simple and incontrovertible truth that knowledge, *as knowledge*, is of necessity opposed to, and distinct from, reality.' Fichte held that reality is given only in immediate experience, or feeling; and feeling is not theoretical but practical. For feeling is passive feeling of the resistance of the *non-ego* to the striving of the *ego* to determine (i.e. limit) it, and though this passivity is indispensable to recognition of a real object, it is not cognizing. Thus, as against Kant, Fichte does not shirk the issue by ascribing the passive affection of sensibility without which knowledge would be impossible to the mysterious influence of the unknown thing-in-itself. For the *ego* posits *itself* as *non-ego*: will is inseparable from thought within the original self-conscious activity of the *ego*, and if it had not the feeling of resistance to its striving to reflect upon, the *ego* could not be self-conscious. Yet knowledge as such is purely formal.

6·4. Hegel's obligation to Fichte is considerable, and had Fichte been able to shape his final views more systematically, it would perhaps have been more openly recognized by Hegel himself. That Fichte's dialectical treatment of his fundamental propositions has markedly influenced Hegel's dialectic will become obvious in Chapters X and XI, and that influence is far from exhausting Hegel's debt. But Hegel

[1] *Fichte*, 1901, pp. 165-6, an excellent account which I have largely followed.

held that though Fichte had recognized that in self-consciousness lay the means of reconciling subject and substance,
yet he had failed to work out the solution. The *non-ego* upon
which the activity of Fichte's *ego* breaks (thereby limiting
itself and diversifying the *non-ego* as its object) is to the *ego*
an *incomprehensible* obstruction. Nevertheless this *non-ego* is
treated by Fichte as produced by the *ego*. The contradiction
is not reconciled. Fichte failed to get completely beyond the
Kantian conception of thought as formal to the notion of
thought as in its full nature a self-constituting *theoretical*
activity containing, but absorbing and transcending, will.
Hence to Hegel the result of Fichte's philosophy seems still
to be subjective idealism.

7. To Schelling Hegel's philosophy of Nature owes a
good deal. But Schelling had, in Hegel's view, ultimately
succeeded only in blurring together subject and object in an
Absolute which Hegel describes as 'a night in which all cows
are black'.

8. The greatness of Hegel largely appears in the con-
tinually vivid presence to his mind of all his predecessors.
He contrives so effectively to diminish the merely casual
element in historical perspective that it is the very great
thinkers of the past, relatively irrespective of their date, who
provide the best introduction to his philosophy. Hence in
the chapter which follows, although Hegel in fact attempted
to interpret the universe through a notion of self-consciousness far more complex than Aristotle's, we will continue to
suppose his thought a direct development of the Aristotelian
philosophy; and in Chapter IX I shall offer a direct comparison of Hegel with Kant rather than with Fichte. In Chapter
XIII, however, I shall approach Hegel mainly through
certain philosophical positions which command support in
this country, because that seems the easiest way to interest
the probable majority of my readers.

VIII
NATURE AND CONCRETE SPIRIT

1. On the Aristotelian *Scala Universi* man stands midway, and his position is puzzling. Whether he look down or up or round about him, he cannot easily relate himself to what he sees; for everywhere he finds ambiguity which he cannot with only Aristotle's aid resolve.

1·1. If he consider to begin with the world below and about him, he finds that the rational activity of man is a form in which the lower forms of that world culminate. If man has reason, and is even essentially and by definition rational, yet he has sentience and he has life. He has also a body within which analysis would reveal simpler and simpler stages of form until the simplest physical form were reached. And these lower forms are not present solely in himself. There are countless sorts of sentient creature besides man, and every lower form than sentience extends more widely than the form next above it: the world below him is far more than the product of his self-analysis, and if he think himself in some sense at the apex of a pyramid, yet he cannot think it the sole purpose of the pyramid to support *his* rational activity. Moreover, the apex flattens to a surface as he looks: he is not the sole occupant, but a man among innumerable other men. In short, both as a developing series of forms which culminates in manhood and also as an environment of inferior and coequal creatures, this world of which he is a fragment seems to be presupposed by and to condition his own peculiar being.

1·2. Nevertheless, and despite these humbling reflections, this whole world which his being presupposes seems after all to be revealed to him, even as a presupposed condition, only as the object and content of his own thinking.

And yet here again he seems to have reached an ambiguous conclusion. For on the one hand his world as the object and content of his own thinking appears to be communicated to him only through the instrumental function of his own sentient body: his thinking seems to presuppose his sentience.

On the other hand, this sentient body comes to him only as part and parcel of the whole object which he thinks: his sentience seems to presuppose his thinking.

1·3. If next he look up to the apex of the pyramid, finding it to be after all above him, his difficulty is not lessened. When he attempts, discontented with Aristotle's seeming severance of God from the world, to reconcile immanence with transcendence, the old ambiguity recurs, and now it is more complex:

(A) God, the pure form above man, seems to presuppose man and to be that in which man and, through man, all the stages of Nature culminate; to be thus as much beyond and above man as Nature seemed beyond and below.

(B) Man knows God only within the content of his own knowing, just as he knew Nature and his fellows only within that content. Moreover, if man thus knows God *and* Nature *and* his fellows, God is so far, like Nature and other men, only a part of the total content of his knowing.

(C) Yet man knows God only by in some sense knowing *with* God, and if God is the ultimate formal cause of Nature and man himself, it can only be in virtue of this same knowing with God that man knows man and Nature as well as God.

(D) Since God *is* self-conscious intelligence, Nature and man must be within God's essence both as knowing and known.

2. Tormented by these puzzles, but comforted perhaps by the thought that after all his very puzzlement betrays the fact that he thinks something and can criticize his own thought, he may make a fresh effort to discover what he is and what he can know.

Two pitfalls he will avoid. (1) With Aristotle's help he will have freed himself from the common-sense notion that he is merely one of a plurality of puzzled men. He will at least realize that thought is not essentially but only incidentally adjectival to a singular individual thinker.[1] (2) He will not suppose (D) to be the whole and sole truth of the matter. For he will see that if he does he will have reduced the conception of the world as in any sense at all other than God to

---

[1] Cf. ch. v, §§ 2·2 ff. above.

an illusion from which there would *ex hypothesi* be nobody left to suffer.[1]

2·1. We may suppose him, then, to mediate between these extremes and endeavour to reconstruct the Aristotelian universe somewhat on the following lines.

He will first exhibit the forms of Nature as a developing series, treating them as the presupposition and condition of human reason. He will, however, remember that if they are the condition of human reason, they yet in some measure also subserve it, and he will be anxious to avoid ascribing to them that self-subsistence which all the lower stages of Aristotle's *Scala Universi* inevitably acquire so far as the Aristotelian God transcends his world and is not its *forma informans*. But we shall find it easier to see what conception of Nature he is likely to reach if we first consider how in general he will interpret the higher stages of the scale, the forms of human spiritual activity.

2·2. In treating the forms of the human spirit[2] his advance upon Aristotle's explicit teaching will be significant. His task will be twofold and not easy. (*a*) He must preserve continuity and show these forms as presupposing and developing from the natural forms, just as each of those presupposed and developed from its predecessor. But in order to do so he must also (*b*) exhibit the forms of human spirit as having Nature for their object or content. For man is higher than Nature not merely because he is conscious, but because he is conscious of Nature. Man's transcendence of Nature is precisely manifest in the presence of Nature as the object of his awareness.[3] Hence man, as he appears to the philosopher, is neither a mere natural existent, nor again—if it be possible

---

[1] The utter severance of God from the world leads to the view that God is unknowable (a Kantian thing-in-itself), and thence by an easy passage to the notion that God is an illusion and only the world real. (D) is the directly opposite view. It is not pantheism—the literal identification of God with any and every *de facto* existent—but rather the 'acosmism' with which Spinoza is charged by Hegel.

[2] 'Mind' would perhaps serve as well, I have preferred 'spirit' as possibly in English slightly the wider term, but there is little to choose between them.

[3] An object within which falls his own body; a point which Aristotle in his doctrine of sense-perception neglects, and lapses accordingly into naïve common sense; cf. ch. iii, §§ 4·5 and 4·8 above.

to imagine such a thing—a bare subjective function, or bundle of functions, in casual commerce with things and indifferent as to what thing may become its object.[1] The forms of man's consciousness divorced from their object or content are nothing; for they are the forms of that content, which is, in Aristotelian terminology, their proximate matter.[2]

2·3. The human spirit, then, in general will be regarded by our philosopher (whom the reader may now assume to be a very thinly disguised Hegel) as essentially a subject in relation to its object. Where there is less than a unity of these two factors there is nothing that can legitimately be called spirit. And certain corollaries follow. Within this concrete unity of subject and object the nature of both subject and object (in general man and Nature) is actual. But the object is content, or proximate matter, and the subject is the unifying form. Hence the philosopher must not only treat subject and object together and in relation; he must treat the unifying subject as dominant in the concrete, and the object as that in which the dominant subject sustains and expresses its own nature. He is, in short, committed to the view that spirit is everywhere in a broad sense self-consciousness,[3] and that every form of it must therefore be treated as an attitude[4] of the subject to an object or content which it unifies, and in which it expresses, whether or not it also recognizes, itself.

3. I have spoken *rudi Minerva* of 'spirit', 'consciousness', and 'self-consciousness'. I have used a vague variety of phrases to express the relation of subject to its object:

---

[1] The second alternative would not in the end differ from the first. Plato as well as Aristotle treats this as obvious; cf. *Republic*, 477 c–d.

[2] The attempt so to divorce them can only lead to the disappearance of any distinction between them (as Plato saw: cf. *Republic*, ibid.), and so to their reduction to a bare subject, Kant's transcendental unity of apperception taken in abstraction, the 'I' which is omnipresent in awareness but can only be defined proleptically with reference to concrete awareness; cf. ch. vii, § 5 above.

[3] It will be remembered that in Aristotle's doctrine of sense-perception the single actualization of object and subject resides in the subject, and self-consciousness is always, though incidentally, present; cf. ch. iii, § 4·7 above.

[4] In the sense not of a static pose but of a directed activity.

'dominance', 'self-expression', 'self-recognition', and so on. I have scarcely distinguished between the terms 'object' and 'content'. In order to make this terminology more precise, we must consider a little how the general character of spirit will differentiate itself for the philosopher in a series of forms or phases, and how from level to level the nature of the object and the attitude of the subject to it will vary.

3·1. The principle will be this. Each phase will be a proximate matter to the phase above it. The total concrete attitude of subject to object, the whole unity of the two related terms in which any given phase consists, will become the object or content of the proximate higher phase, which will accordingly exhibit a fresh attitude of the subject to a fresh object. It is not merely that 'we rise on stepping-stones of our dead selves'; for the 'dead' self, as an entire concrete attitude of subject to object, is 'dead' only in so far as it has ceased to be the level at which the subject 'lives'. The 'dead' self 'lives' again freshly informed; it 'lives' reduced to a state of instrumentality, but thereby exalted and redintegrated with the subject, at the higher level to which the subject's activity has raised it.

We shall see how Hegel elaborates upwards on this principle from what may be roughly called 'feeling'—even from something lower than that—where no definite relation of subject and object is yet present, and the 'object' is rather a 'content' scarce distinguishably one with what can hardly as yet be called a subject. Meanwhile certain points are worth note.

3·11. The self-consciousness of ordinary experience is, on Hegel's view, a quite transparent revelation of self-diremption which does not destroy but, on the contrary, preserves and sustains self-identity. And within the limits of everyday experience this real identity of self in difference takes a number of perfectly familiar forms: self-control and self-contempt, self-knowledge and self-deceit, and so forth. But in the present context self-consciousness is a term demanding the very broadest and most general interpretation. It must be stretched to include not only bare feeling and perhaps something even less than that, but also phases of spirit in which the attitude of the subject is a seemingly

intransigent repulsion of an alien object: that realistical attitude of natural science and of common sense (if that signifies
any one attitude[1]) which even detaches itself and accords its
object a status of total independence of and indifference to
the subject.

3.12. Hence, save at the level of philosophic thinking, the
subject is never fully aware that its object is its own lower
self transcended—that its activity is essentially self-reconstitutive. In none of its lower phases[2] is the subject aware of
its object as containing within itself the series of yet lower
phases from which it has in fact developed. The object of its
awareness is to the subject only its *proximate* lower self,[3] and
in some phases the subject must even necessarily repudiate
the suggestion that the object is the subject's self at all. In
natural science, for example, the subject is aware that it is
working on the basis of its own experience (which the philosopher will recognize as its proximate lower self), but it is
the distinctive characteristic of natural science to regard its
own activity not as self-reconstitutive but as the coming to
know better an independent object-world already less perfectly apprehended through sense.

3.2. If nothing be spirit which is less than a concrete of
subject and object within which subject is dominant, the
philosopher must interpret any phase or level of spirit in one
sense from within; for it is his business to exhibit the subject's view of itself, of its object, and of the relation between
them, and he could not do this if he had not himself the
capacity for experience at the level of spirit which he is
attempting to explain. On the other hand, he cannot, in interpreting any phase of spirit, be actually at the level he interprets. To interpret is to transcend; to philosophize is to be at
a philosophical and no other level. Nor, if it satisfy both these
conditions, does interpretation falsify. For any given level of
experience is fulfilled in being transcended; its interpretation
is its truth in the sense of its own real, developed self.[4]

---

[1] Cf. ch. i, § 1.2 above.
[2] i.e. in none of the phases of Subjective Spirit; cf. § 6 below.
[3] Or rather, perhaps, its lower self *only* as proximate; not recognized as a
stage in which lower stages culminate.
[4] Cf. ch. ii, § 2, on definition; also ch. xiv below.

3·21. Spirit is thus a subject which from phase to phase reconstitutes, or comes to fuller possession of, its own nature. Of this self-reconstitutive principle philosophy is the palmary instance, because to philosophy alone the principle itself becomes evident in and as the whole developing series of phases which, in Hegel's view, is crowned by philosophy. Many lower phases are not distinctively interpretative (theoretical), and no lower phase is a complete self-reconstituting of the subject without unabsorbed residue, so to say, of the lower self—indeed in some cases the imperfect transcendence of the lower self may even, as we shall see, bring it about that the subject takes itself to be at once on two levels of experience, the higher of which even seems to lack something which the lower possessed. Nevertheless any phase is an activity self-reconstitutive and directed primarily upon its proximate lower self.

3·3. We cannot yet specify these phases in detail, but the principle can be roughly exemplified at the level where thought first transcends sense. Here thought is much as I have described it in speaking of common sense.[1] Hegel calls it 'Understanding' (*Verstand*), following Kant's use of the term. Understanding claims to do better what sense has done; to exhibit the content of sense in a truer form, and so far to transcend it. Yet thought at the level of Understanding is abstract and general, stripped naked of the richness of sense. The subject seems to itself to think, but at the same time to be still at the level of sense function, and to be able to purify its thinking of sensuous support only at the cost of a proportionate severity of abstraction. Nevertheless thought does begin as a reconstitution of sensuous experience, and it is upon our perceived world that our thinking is primarily directed. Moreover, if to provide a further example we subdivide within sense function, we discover that though imagination develops and transcends mere perception, yet this development is barely more than a *persistence* of *perceptum* and percipient subject.[2] We are able—or it is rather the symptom of our impotence—to imagine, to perceive directly, and perhaps even to experience in the form of mere sensation, the same content in one and the same act. Yet

[1] Ch. i, § 1·2. [2] Cf. ch. v, § 2 above.

within such complex experience each higher phase, though it fails to absorb totally the lower, is essentially the reconstituting of it.[1]

3·4. Thus in order to interpret any level of spirit, the philosopher must (1) be able to experience at that level, and be able, as it were, to speak authoritatively for the subject which is at that level; and he must also (2) have raised himself to the higher level of philosophic experience. That is to say (1) he cannot observe from without. To attempt to do so would be to adopt the attitude of the subject in natural science, so placing himself at a level of experience where he can do nothing but reconstitute the world of sense-perception as a world of rudimentary thought (Understanding), as a world of scientific laws or principles. For the distinctive feature of the Understanding is that the subject takes its object to be external and alien to itself.[2] Hence the philosopher, instead of adopting this self-defeating procedure,[3] must so far work from within as to grasp the subject's attitude to its object at the level which is to be interpreted,

[1] Because the Understanding and such grades of sense function as are developed beyond mere sensation all have in common what, if it be erroneously exalted to the position of a philosophic standpoint, must be called a realist attitude towards their object, and because (in a manner not clear to the experient subject) no one of them functions wholly free of the rest, it is impossible to abstain altogether from describing the procedure of them all as if it were the same. So Hegel, though in the *Philosophy of Spirit* he most carefully distinguishes and orders them, yet will use much the same language in criticizing the procedure of *Verstand* in natural science and of *Vorstellen*, which means in Hegel roughly 'perceptual imagination' or 'imaging', and again of the *räsonnieren* of common sense. In the latter part of this book I find myself compelled to use the same seemingly ambiguous phraseology because I am there in effect criticizing the same sort of experience in different contexts. 'Empirical thinking' is perhaps the best general term.

[2] The natural scientist can reconstitute the perceived world as a 'scientific' world, and natural science, as a fresh attitude of subject to object, is an essential phase in the reconstruction of sense-perception. But the natural scientist cannot explain sense-perception, or any other level of spirit, as a part of his object. For in the object-world of natural science there is *ex hypothesi* no subject.

[3] Self-defeating if supposed to be philosophic. But Hegel allows that what is properly a philosophic subject-matter can be treated at the level of Understanding with results useful, even indispensable, to philosophy. Formal logic, for example, so treats thought; cf. § 5·7 below.

doing so by virtue of his own capacity for experience at that level. But (2) he must also by virtue of having transcended that level look back on it, as it were, and exhibit it in its place in the developing series within which it is a phase.

3·41. Clearly his task in dealing with phases low on the scale will not be easy. His capacity for sensation and what other lower forms of experience there may be has never been actualized with the comparative purity of, for example, his volitional or his aesthetic experience. He is in constant danger of sophisticating sensation, because man does not ever simply sensate; and of any lower phases this is true *a fortiori*. Still, there is no other source of evidence which he can tap,[1] no other method which he can pursue.

4. We can now perhaps profitably pause to look back and see a little more clearly how the philosopher could come to apprehend Nature.[2] How far, we may ask, was it this same method which served him when he descended below spirit to the forms of Nature with which the scale of spiritual forms is by him asserted to be continuous?

At least it is clear that he cannot adopt the attitude of an external observer. Whatever use he may make of natural science (and doubtless it will be considerable), he can no more fix himself at the level of the scientific Understanding in order to interpret Nature than he was able to do so in order to explain a level of spirit. To do so in either case would be to renounce his philosophic activity.

4·1. Is his interpretation of Nature, then, subject to any condition analogous to the first condition of interpreting a phase of spirit? The answer seems to be in the affirmative: as the philosopher must himself be capable of, for example, sense-perception and will in order to explain them, so he must be himself natural in order to explain Nature. If he did not

---

[1] This is, of course, not to say that he is confined for evidence to his 'private' sensations. He can find it in other men's expression of sensation. But that is because at no level wholly, and least of all at a philosophic level, is his experience 'private' in the sense of an atomically isolated subject's experience. That the subject should take itself for one among an indefinite plurality of subjects is merely a distinctive feature of certain levels of spirit. Cf. ch. v, § 2·2 above.

[2] Only a quite provisional account of Hegel's conception of Nature can be given while his logic has not been discussed.

experience his physical body as at once in some sense himself and at the same time continuous with a natural world distinct from himself, he could know nothing of Nature. Without the mediation of his body he could not be conscious at all of that opposition of mind and Nature which Descartes erected into absolute unmediated opposition. He finds in the lowest phases of spirit a subject[1] coming to itself as a nisus of self-assertion against something non-spiritual and other than itself, but as a nisus, too, to dominate and absorb that 'other' within itself. There at once he touches Nature.

4·2. He can now look for a condition to fulfil analogous to the second condition of interpreting spirit. Spirit in its every phase is a reduction of its lower self to object, but also thereby a self-reconstitution; and from that the philosopher will infer that this non-spiritual 'other' which the subject is struggling at once to distinguish and to dominate is genuinely analogous to the lower self which spirit in its higher phases makes its object and content. Moreover, if he is assailed by doubt and seeks at this low level for a self utterly separate from this non-spiritual 'other', he soon discovers that that which struggles and that with which it struggles are closely interfused, and that he can find no feature or content to constitute any such separate self. The principle that there is spirit wherever there is a concrete attitude—however rudimentary—of subject to object cannot, as it seems, be abandoned even when the object-term of the concrete seems at first sight to be utterly non-spiritual. He will therefore conclude that the two factors, the struggling subject and the non-spiritual 'other' with which it struggles, have emerged —or rather, perhaps, are precisely the process of emerging— from a level at which they were not yet distinct; in short, that they emerge from Nature.

4·21. Thus Nature as the philosopher infers it will not be other than spirit with that precise character of 'otherness' in which its non-spiritual 'other' opposes the subject at the lowest levels of spirit; nor, indeed, with precisely that 'other-

---

[1] The terms 'subject' and 'object' are here used to signify what are in fact only their distant analogues. The same is true of many other terms used in this section, e.g. 'struggle' and 'dominance'. We are still below any definite distinction between theoretical and practical.

ness' with which Nature confronts common sense, or natural science, or the subject at any other level of spirit. For the philosopher has reached Nature—and made good its continuity with spirit—as that which is presupposed by spiritual experience as a whole, not as the object correlated with the subject in any particular phase of spirit. Nature is for him essentially that in which no subject-object relation has emerged, and as such Nature may seem to be more utterly other than and alien to spirit than it is as the object correlated with the subject in any particular phase; for whereas spirit is a subject always in its relation to its object related to itself, Nature as such is essentially external to itself. Yet Nature must be in some sense an object of spirit at the level of philosophic thinking. Hence to the philosopher the absence of subject-object relation, the self-externality of Nature, is a *determinate* absence, a significant privation. If it were not, 'self-externality' would be a meaningless phrase; Nature totally abstracted from spirit could not be anything. Nature is, then, for philosophy not the simply non-spiritual, but the pre-spiritual from which spirit *must* emerge. There is in Nature nothing positive which it does not possess by virtue of its approximation to spirit. To suppose that Nature is in its own right positive is to remain, attempting vainly to philosophize, at the level of Understanding; to seek in Nature some inner secret of its own is to lose oneself in a baseless and futile mysticism.

4·3. Thus the conditions of interpreting Nature philosophically *are* analogous to the conditions which govern a philosophic interpretation of spirit. But it is important to observe the difference between them. Because he is himself natural and has a body continuous with the rest of the natural world, the philosopher can in a sense speak authoritatively for Nature. But in so doing he is not speaking for a subject at a certain level, for Nature in general is self-external and below the level at which the distinction of subject and object emerges. Nature, as Hegel puts it, is only *an sich* and not (as any level of spirit is) also *für sich*: it is not yet anything for itself. Hence for philosophic interpretation of Nature, *an sich* is equivalent to *für uns*. There is no such thing as self-dependent Nature *an sich* apart from spirit. Nature, being nothing for itself because it is subjectless, is nothing but the pre-spiritual, which must find its subjectivity in spirit.[1] Thus the pre-spiritual falls in some sense within spirit: the non-spiritual, which spirit in its lowest phases is trying to 'dominate' and 'absorb', is *en fin de compte* spirit itself.

5. This gives the philosopher his general conception of Nature as such, but it gives him no more. He has so far only the bare principle on which he must work in order to differentiate and grade Nature in the phases of its development towards spirit.

5·1. It is well at this point to remember that the revelation to the subject of what I have called 'a non-spiritual other' begins in the lowest phases of spirit as the merest germ of self-distinction, and only comes to be definite in sense-perception and in the succeeding phase of Understanding, where thought begins as a reconstitution of the perceived world and elaborates itself *par excellence* in natural science. Throughout this progress Nature (for the progressing subject) gradually develops determinate features, not as pre-spiritual (as for the philosopher Nature is) but as an object which the subject confronts as its non-spiritual 'other'. To the scientific Understanding—the first purely theoretical level of spirit—Nature is definitely external to the understanding subject, an object correlated with the subject but taken to be independent of it; and for this scientific Understanding Nature divides into roughly separable subject-matters of inquiry. Of these various subject-matters one may seem more abstract and another more concrete, so as to suggest some sort of developing order—as, for example, between physics and biology—but the distinctive character of system as it appears in the object-world of the Understanding is differentiation in co-ordinate classes,[2] and in laws of mechanical *ab extra* necessitation which do not express natural change as development.[3]

5·2. These sciences of Nature are not philosophy, but

[1] Nature as thus *für uns* is not Nature as the object of the scientific Understanding, for which see next section.

[2] Cf. ch. iv above.

[3] In general, a conception of cause as an Aristotelian efficient cause divorced from the formal and final moments of causation.

they do provide the only possible material for a philosophy
of Nature. Hegel's view—never perfectly clear—seems to
be this. Not only can the philosopher interpret Understanding in general as a level of spirit, as an attitude of subject to object which he can himself experience, and which as
a philosopher he transcends; he can also, if he can first
'understand' it, interpret the detail of its object—the
scientific world of Nature—from his own philosophical
level. And this 'understanding' of Nature conditions, in the
sense that it subserves, the philosophy of Nature. That,
indeed, follows from the conception of philosophic interpretation with which Hegel is working. For, in general, the
first condition which the interpreter must fulfil is to have
been at the level which he would interpret, and the second
is to transcend it, to elevate himself to the level of a philosophic experience which is the truth of the level to be interpreted. But this self-elevation must clearly pass through all
intervening levels. And all these intervening levels must
obviously contribute to the philosophic interpretation.
Hence, the philosopher both can and must 'understand' the
world of natural science in order to interpret Nature philosophically.

5·21. It might be objected that this proves too much.
How, it might be asked, can the philosopher of Nature, on
this account, ignore (1) the levels prior to natural science and
the Understanding, and (2) any levels which may intervene
between natural science and philosophy? Why, at the least,
should not any one of the latter help him as much as—nay,
even more than—natural science in the interpretation of
Nature?

The answer to (1) is that the level of natural science is the
first level of spirit which is itself explicitly a theoretical interpretation of its object, and that levels prior to this do not
openly reveal Nature as antithesis to spirit, because they are
themselves still too natural. What they do reveal to the
philosopher is the *prius* of the Understanding as itself a
phase of spirit.

The answer to (2) is (*a*) that Nature as the pre-spiritual
transcended in spirit does enter into the subject-matter
of philosophic interpretation at all the intervening levels of

spirit. Practical activity, art, and religion, which for Hegel comprise these intervening levels, are still phases in spirit's 'conquest' of the natural. And this foreknowledge, as it were, of Nature's destiny does operate when the philosopher constructs a philosophy of Nature. But (*b*), as in the levels prior to natural science Nature had not clearly emerged over against the subject, so at the levels above the Understanding Nature is partly reabsorbed into spirit; it has won a significance which is not that of Nature as such. At the lower levels of practical activity, for example, Nature is a world which the human spirit can alter and subordinate, a kingdom whose laws it can outwit if not defy; at the higher practical levels Nature is *for* man a stuff *within* him of which he must make himself; in aesthetic activity Nature is beautiful. Nowhere at these levels is there Nature as such. Hence it is *par excellence* the explicitly non-spiritual world of natural science to which the philosopher must look for detail to reinterpret in his account of Nature as such, of Nature as *an sich* and *für uns*, of Nature as the essentially pre-spiritual.

5.3. In interpreting Nature as such the philosopher will proceed as follows. He has already recognized that the lowest level of spirit implies a pre-spiritual, self-external Nature, and that systematized Nature to which the man of science accords independent reality has in fact emerged as a development of that pre-spiritual Nature. Hence he infers that the systematized object of natural science does imperfectly reflect what that pre-spiritual Nature must be. Nature to the natural scientist is expressly non-spiritual, because it is assumed by him (consciously or unconsciously) to be real in independence of himself apprehending it. But if Nature be taken not as non-spiritual but as pre-spiritual, then the system of differentiation by co-ordinate classes, and what in general might be called the 'dead-levelness' of natural science, will give place to a Nature differentiated and graded in phases through which its self-externality diminishes as it approximates to spirit.

5.4. By thus accepting and reinterpreting the results of natural science Hegel constructs a philosophy of Nature as a developing series which ascends from space and time to animal life. The question how far this construction is justified in principle or successful in detail must await further discussion, but it is worth while for a moment to consider it as an effort to solve an Aristotelian problem.

5·5. The sheer self-externality of Nature as such is closely akin to Aristotle's primary matter, the 'alogical' principle of indefinite multiplicity, which is also sheer privation; and when Hegel begins his Philosophy of Nature with Space and Time we are reminded that the dynamic aspect of primary matter is to Aristotle a sheer potentiality, which is at once brute necessity and sheer contingency.[1] But Aristotle had not altogether succeeded in coming to terms with matter and contingency. They seem in his system to remain after all an intractable residue, testifying scandalously against the Platonic and Aristotelian principle that the real and the intelligible are one. For Aristotle, despite his hierarchical conception of the universe, did not quite clearly distinguish between (*a*) common sense and natural science as the investigation of a non-spiritual object, and (*b*) a philosophic theory of Nature as the pre-spiritual.

5·6. One side of this antithesis, and only one, was revealed more clearly when with the decay of Aristotelianism natural science began to repudiate teleology.[2] But a definite complementary treatment of Nature as pre-spiritual only became possible when the problem of substance and subject had been reformulated.[3] This treatment, foreshadowed in Leibniz but conspicuously absent from Kant, appears confusedly in Schelling and more clearly in Hegel. For Hegel Nature as such is self-external and utterly contingent, but 'Nature as such' means to Hegel Nature not as it is for sense-perception and Understanding, but as it is for philosophic thought. An indefinite multiplicity of singulars which come to be and pass away is an object strictly correlative to sense-perception. Divorce it from the percipient subject and whatever then be left it will not be that multiplicity.[4] Sheer

---

[1] Cf. ch. iii, § 6·2 above.

[2] Descartes was far less conscious of any such antithesis than Aristotle, and even Kant in the *Critique of Judgment* offers with one hand the possibility of interpreting Nature teleologically and withdraws it with the other.

[3] Cf. ch. vii, §§ 5 ff. above.

[4] As Aristotle discovered; cf. ch. iii, § 4·5 above.

contingency coupled with brute necessity belongs only to the peculiar object-world of the Understanding, a world in which objects seem rather to behave contingently than to be in their own nature contingent, since they are for the Understanding *ex hypothesi* real things. These are ways of apprehending which the philosopher must take account of if he would interpret sense-perception and Understanding, but they are not *his* ways of apprehending. The contingency which he sees in Nature is not that intractable residue in its object which defies the Understanding, any more than it is something which he can dismiss as illusion. It is, if we like to call it so, an essential contingency; but philosophy, though it can and must examine the distinction of contingent and necessary as it appears to the Understanding, can make no distinction between a contingent and a necessary, an essential and an accidental element, in its own object.[1] The contingency, or self-externality, of Nature as such is only 'essential' in the sense that it distinctively characterizes Nature as that pre-spiritual other which must fall within the self-distinguishing and self-integrating activity which spirit is. The approximation of Nature to individuality, the gradual reduction of self-externality to system which the philosopher detects, signify for him only the progress of spirit's self-integration. As natural science advances the philosophy of Nature advances, and there is even in the scientist himself, maybe, a touch of prophetic insight upon which the philosopher must seize; but scientific discovery can never lead the philosopher to speculative knowledge of an object as that object rests defined in terms of the Understanding.

5.7. There thus emerge certain characteristics of the Understanding, as Hegel sees it, which it may be well here to sum up.

(*a*) Understanding always takes its object to be independent of, and indifferent to, its own thinking; but it does not absorb without residue the lower levels of experience which it transcends.[2]

(*b*) In its ordinary exercise it functions without self-

---

[1] Hegel's categories of Essence contain a moment of contingency, but the dialectical movement of those categories is not contingent.

[2] Cf. § 3.3 above.

reflection. In natural science, for example, it consists in a resolute effort to expel the contingency which common sense takes more or less for granted, but this effort is confined to interpretation of the sensuous object-world.

(c) The germ of a more developed form of thinking is in it, since its truth lies at levels above it with which it is therefore continuous. And this germ is not wholly latent. Not only are there in it, even in its exercise in mathematics and natural science, what may be called gleams of Reason, but also it can reflect in a rudimentary manner upon its own nature. But in this self-reflection it will still view itself as an object just as 'detached' and indifferent as the object of its ordinary exercise. Both formal logic and empirical psychology are products of the Understanding in this function of elementary self-reflection.[1]

(d) The Understanding is at once presupposed by and absorbed in reason. 'The merits and rights of the mere Understanding must before all be admitted. And that merit lies in the fact that apart from Understanding there is no fixity or accuracy in the region either of theory or practice.' To say nothing of conduct, neither art nor religion can dispense with it, and it is the primary characteristic of philosophical speculation that 'every thought shall be grasped in its full precision, and nothing allowed to remain vague and indefinite'.[2]

(e) Yet Understanding is not a level of experience at which genuine philosophy is possible. When Krug offered his pen for philosophical deduction, Hegel was irritated by the naïveté, and replied that for the present he had something better to do.[3] It has not always been understood in what Krug's naïveté consisted. Krug was in fact suggesting that an object of sense-perception ought on Hegel's theory to be philosophically explicable and yet remain an object of sense-perception and Understanding. Hegel's answer had been given some ten years before in the Phänomenologie des Geistes.[4]

6. In attempting in §§ 2·2–2·3 of this chapter to sketch Hegel's treatment of spirit in more or less direct relation to Aristotle's I have illustrated it chiefly with examples such as

---

[1] See ch. x, §§ 3–4·3 below.
[3] ΦN, § 250.
[2] EL, § 80, Zusatz.
[4] Phän. JE, ii, p. 86.

sensation, sense-perception, and Understanding, which Hegel regards as phases of spirit logically preceding the development of will. They are in fact phases belonging to the first part of Hegel's Philosophy of Spirit, which he entitles Subjective Spirit. This is not to say that many of Hegel's forms of Subjective Spirit are not lower analogues of will—and indeed of activities higher than will—but the general characteristic of Subjective Spirit is that the subject finds a presupposed world confronting it, and the highest achievement of Subjective Spirit, unless I misunderstand Hegel, is the elaboration of the Understanding in mathematics and natural science, a 'detached' thinking of an alien object.

6·1. The phases of spirit which next succeed are practical. Spirit, in the general form of will, gradually appropriates the world it has discovered confronting it. Law (in the sense of legality), the ethics of conscience, and political philosophy culminating in world-history are the main subdivisions of practical activity, and Hegel groups them under the head of Objective Spirit. In Subjective Spirit the emphasis is in general on modes of consciousness, and Hegel's concern is to show that these without their content are nothing. In the succeeding realm of Objective Spirit it is the objective aspect, the binding law or the political institution, which first strikes one, and Hegel's effort is therefore to show that these live only in spirit, and are nothing apart from the subject which realizes itself in them.

In the detail of his moral and political philosophy, and in the close connexion which he maintains between them, Hegel is perhaps more directly inspired by Plato and Aristotle than in any other part of his system, although world-history in Hegel's sense is not a Greek conception, and although in Hegel the sharp Aristotelian distinction of art (in the sense of craft) from conduct is considerably softened. Hegel envisages all practical activity from a more or less ethical point of view, and he is so far nearer to Plato than to Aristotle. On the other hand, to Plato moral, religious, and philosophical activity are still barely distinct, and Plato's articulation of values, as Hegel sees it, takes shape as a revolt against the predominantly aesthetic colouring of Greek spiritual experience.[1] To Aristotle is due the clear conception (which he probably reached fairly late in life) of an ethical experience not specifically religious, but Aristotle still does not clearly differentiate between philosophy and the religious consciousness.

6·2. Above Objective Spirit come levels which the philosopher must recognize as forms of experience wherein the human spirit, progressively self-conscious, begins to be explicitly aware of more than Nature and its own mere human self; forms whose content is the divine activity. Such experience is possible only if human experience is transcended to become an element within the content of the divine experience; only if, as man comes to know himself better, his knowing is in some sense a knowing *with* God.[2] Hegel marks the advent of these levels as the transition from finite to infinite spirit. He entitles them 'Art', 'Revealed Religion', and 'Philosophy'. He is thereby expanding the Aristotelian 'First Philosophy' (for which 'theology' was a synonym) with what he conceived to be the essential content of Christian revelation, and supplementing it with aesthetic experience.

Of aesthetic experience the Greeks had no clear and distinct conception. Plato on the whole shared the Greek error of mistaking technique for the essence of the fine arts,[3] but the significance of his revolt against fine art was, according to Hegel, this. In the Greek notion of absolute spirit aesthetic, religious, and philosophic experience were found by Plato more or less undifferentiated. The Greek spirit was still, therefore, at a level which is more properly to be called aesthetic than religious or philosophical.[4] Plato, beginning to articulate these differences,[5] is at once in conflict with the predominantly aesthetic Greek *Weltanschauung*. Plato recognizes that aesthetic experience, though sensuous in form, is rational,[6] but he sets his face against the notion that

---

[1] See following section.

[2] Cf. § 1·3 above.

[3] In his *Principles of Art* Prof. Collingwood treats admirably of the Greek conception of art; see esp. pp. 17–19 and 42–52.

[4] Cf. JE, xiii, Aesth., ii, pp. 16–17.

[5] Especially in the *Philebus*.

[6] e.g. in *Phaedrus, Symposium, Hippias Major*. Cf. JE, xviii, HΦ, pp. 296–7.

it is the highest form of rational experience. 'Plato', says Hegel, 'did not banish art from his state; he merely declined to let it remain as God.'[1] This is true, I think, with the reservation that Plato's attack on art is embittered by the fact that he still shares the Greek confusion of fine art with craft. Aristotle in the *Poetics* did a little towards dispelling this confusion, but to him beauty was quite evidently neither so precious nor so dangerous as it was to Plato.

6·3. Hegel groups Art, Revealed Religion, and Philosophy as Absolute Spirit. Subject and object, in Nature merely prefigured, in Subjective and Objective Spirit developing in a reciprocal relation which changes from phase to phase, approach in art and religion, and in philosophy attain, a singleness above division.

Absolute Spirit as philosophy is thus the fully self-conscious and self-conditioning—or, as Hegel calls it, 'free'—activity with which Aristotle identifies God. But it is not divorced from Nature and the stages of spirit which it crowns. They are its content, its lower self, of which its activity *is* the transcending.

6·4. This identification of the highest phase of Absolute Spirit with philosophy has repelled many thinkers even among confessed idealists; Bradley and Croce, for example, have from different points of view rejected it. But if philosophic interpretation to be true must *be* the ultimate real nature, the final and formal cause, of what it interprets—if, to put it negatively, thinking so far as it is not one with its object is not knowledge but ignorance—then this identification is inevitable.

6·41. The position cannot here be fully discussed, but certain consequences of it must not be left in doubt. It entails the view that philosophic experience is as such the experience of intrinsic value, presenting the sharpest contrast to the thinking of the natural scientist and the mathematician. Hegel must and does maintain that 'value judgement' is not the capricious subjective expression of a private feeling of enjoyment or approval (or the reverse)—not something merely 'emotive' and alogical, as on any intellec-

---

[1] *ΦH*, Lasson's ed. 1920, vol. iii, p. 639. I cannot find any similar passage in JE.

tualist conception of thought which finds in, e.g., mathematics the truest type of thinking, it is bound to become—but the only thinking that can attain to genuine objectivity. That is in brief Hegel's distinction between Understanding and Reason. Thus if philosophy is passionless, it is above passion; neither the servant of the passions, nor dispassionate and aloof. If it is 'theory', it is not detached reflection subserving some spiritual activity other than itself, for it would then be a special science; nor is it an activity independent of other activities, for it would then be otiose.

6·42. This conception of thought is essentially Greek. It recalls Plato's certain faith in philosophy as the supreme way of life, and it recalls the ideal of θεωρία with which Aristotle concludes the *Nicomachean Ethics*. But there is a considerable difference between Hegel and the Greeks. In their speculation the special natures of aesthetic and religious experience have scarcely crystallized to a problem, and when Aristotle loosens θεωρία from practical thinking as Plato had hardly begun to do,[1] he appears, though nowhere quite openly, to rank the thinking of the special scientist with, or close to, theology rather than below practical thinking. Moreover, an ascetic impulse sometimes moved Plato to regard philosophy as a liberation made possible by the repression rather than by the 'sublimation' of subrational elements in the human soul. That and the fascination of mathematics—the factor most difficult to estimate in his speculation—led him into some confusion between two dissimilar sorts of thinking.[2] In Aristotle both these tendencies are less strong, but sufficient trace of them survives to afford a partial excuse for the charge—in the main unjust—of intellectualism, which has so often been urged against Greek philosophy. But to call Hegel intellectualist is the shallowest of all criticisms. Whether his be a true ordering of man's spiritual activities may be questioned,

---

[1] Cf. ch. v, § 4·2 above.

[2] It was evidently Plato's hope to blend in a mathematical philosophy the accuracy made possible by the precise 'finish' (ἀκρίβεια) of a mathematical subject-matter with the truth realized in the experience of the good. Aristotle was not enamoured of mathematics, but he never makes quite clear the relation between ἀκρίβεια and ἀλήθεια.

but that Hegel held speculative thought to be null and void unless in principle it absorb within itself *all* content is beyond doubt. Man is rational; if he divide his allegiance he is not fully a man.

6·43. Before we reject Hegel's position we should reflect upon two points.

In the first place, we should ask ourselves whether there is any real alternative to the Hegelian view that 'thought in its immanent determinations and the true nature of things are one and the same content',[1] except sheer empiricism, the doctrine which denies that we can learn by thinking and offers no explanation of how we learn at all. We should consider whether upon careful criticism any half-way position does not turn out to entail a claim to knowledge from which its own premises preclude it. We should ask, in short, upon what valid grounds thought can disclaim supremacy among the forms of experience; how it can know its place if that place be not the highest.

Secondly, we should reflect that Hegel's view of philosophy affords the individual philosopher no excuse for pride. Rather it compels the humbling reflection that philosophy demands in a man so rich a touch of universality that few of us can hope to grace our profession. History shows countless heroes of action, fewer but still many great artists, a handful of prophets who have brought a new epoch about by cleansing men's hearts, rarely indeed a philosopher who has changed the face of the world by the sole impetus of his thought. Not many of us count, but if we think with Hegel we must not look for the fault in the nature of philosophic thinking.[2]

On the other hand, philosophy is no more the exclusive business of professionals than is art or religion. If there were not in every man, however intermittently he feels it, and however inadequately he interprets it, the nisus towards attaining a total and unreserved self-consciousness, there would be no professional philosophers.

7. It is now perhaps scarcely necessary to observe that in Hegel's view the progress from phase to phase through the

---

[1] LL, i, p. 39.
[2] Cf. also Kant, KRV, B, 866–7.

forms of Nature and spirit is not in time. It may be somehow reflected in the development of a human being's mind between birth and maturity, or in an historical progress from barbarism to culture, but any such processes which there may be presuppose this progress and point to it for their own explanation. The *object* of spirit in some phases is temporal —biography and history may then fall within it—but in Hegel's view Space is the first and Time the second form in, or rather as, which self-external Nature is expressed. Hence no phase of Concrete Spirit as such (i.e. no concrete active attitude of subject to object) is a temporal process, and the phases of Nature and Concrete Spirit as a continuous developing series are no more successive in time than they are juxtaposed in space. To suppose that they are is to suppose that you can force them into the object-world of a prephilosophic phase of spirit. It is an attempt to philosophize at the level of Understanding, rather like trying to pack up a coat into one of its own pockets.

8. This train of reflection from an Aristotelian starting-point may serve to introduce in barest outline the Philosophy of Nature and the Philosophy of Spirit as these are contained in Hegel's *Encyclopaedia*. But Hegel does not regard philosophies of Nature and Spirit as covering the whole field of philosophical activity. In Nature there is contingency, and although it is Hegel's view that this contingency is not a cloak for ignorance but a character which, *qua* prespiritual, Nature possesses essentially, yet if Nature were its only object then philosophic thought could not be wholly one with its object. And in the Philosophy of Spirit contingency diminishes, but it does not entirely vanish. It is, however, logic which is *par excellence* philosophy. In logic alone, as Hegel conceives it, thought moves free of contingency as such.

IX

CATEGORIES

1. THE relation of Hegel's Logic to the philosophies of Nature and, as I shall henceforth call it, Concrete Spirit is a crucial problem of Hegelian exegesis. At present I can only state it with merest generality. Nor will Aristotle any longer serve us as a starting-point. The Aristotelian logic is in Hegel's view a natural history of finite thought;[1] i.e. it presents a set of fixed thought-forms elicited by the reflection of Understanding upon the thinking of natural science and common sense.[2] Though it performed a great service, it was not, he says, the real nerve of Aristotle's speculation.[3] Hegel perhaps owed more to the general structure of Aristotle's philosophical system than to that of any other thinker, but in logic *eo nomine* he is indebted more to Plato's later dialogues than to Aristotle's *Organon*.

1·1. In the philosophies of Nature and Concrete Spirit the philosopher has tried, so to say, to unroll the content, the proximate matter, which has gone to the making of that form of conscious spirit which philosophy is. He has set it forth as a developing series of phases which rise through Nature up to man, traversing first man's subjective modes of consciousness and then the objective activities in which they are concretely developed. He has shown that in the forms of Absolute Spirit man has become explicitly conscious of something more than himself which makes him what he is. Here the centre of gravity, so to speak, begins to shift. The artist enjoys the Absolute in a sensuous medium, and he does not stand over against it simply perceiving, or understanding, or altering his object: his 'creation' and his 'vision' are an explicit self-consciousness and not a finite activity. The essence of Revealed Religion is the self-diremption of God into God (the God of religion) and man: religion is more nearly the divine activity than is, for example, moral conduct. But even Revealed Religion remains dual-centred, still

---

[1] Or of thought as appearance only.
[2] Cf. ch. viii, § 5·7 (*c*) above.
[3] Cf. ch. iv, § 4·5 above.

a human experience in an imaginative medium. Only in philosophy can man concentrate himself upon that aspect or moment of experience in which it shows itself to be centred in God; to be after all not a mere moment but the truth and totality of experience. And so far as the philosopher cares for nothing but to make explicit that moment—so far as he sets himself really to think—he is a logician. It is *par excellence* as a logician that man exemplifies the highest phase of Absolute Spirit, Philosophy.

1·2. The relation of the Logic to the Philosophies of Nature and Concrete Spirit is, as I have said, not quickly to be settled. But this much now becomes clear. The logician's industry is justified only on the assumption that the divine activity is the *forma informans* really immanent in the phases of Nature and Concrete Spirit despite their seeming contingency. Since, then, this divine activity is self-conscious intelligence, the 'eternal moment' which the logician finds in the phases of Nature and Concrete Spirit can be nothing but a partial self-definition on the part of this self-conscious intelligence; on the part of God, or, as Hegel usually prefers to call it in a philosophical context, Absolute Spirit. These partial self-definitions of Absolute Spirit are the categories, or, as he likes better to call them, *Denkbestimmungen*, of Hegel's logic.

2. Lest this conception of logic may seem extravagant and not very intelligible, it is better perhaps here to make a fresh start and approach the Hegelian category from the level of common sense.

If we examine the judgements which we make in characterizing the objects, the individual 'things', of ordinary experience,[1] we find more than one way of distinguishing *rudi Minerva* the types of predicate which we affirm or deny of the logical subject. We can, for example, use the grammatical distinction of substantive from adjective in order to express a formal difference between predicates such as 'dog' or 'star' or 'triangle' predicatively employed, and predicates such as 'malodorous' or 'red' or 'triangular', which are adjectival and so directly predicational in form. But of more

[1] Throughout the following sections the reader should bear in mind p. 66, footnote 1.

immediate importance to us is a division of predicates in terms of content. We may begin by classing together the predicates of empirical judgements, subdividing roughly into (a) the more concrete and sensuous, such as 'dog' or 'malodorous', and (b) the more abstract, such as 'triangle' or 'linear', which are not precisely sensuous, though they have a close reference to sense.

2·1. These distinctions of course make no sort of claim to be exhaustive, and in erecting them we are only doing crudely and barely what many natural historians of thought besides Aristotle have done with indefatigable ingenuity. We are reflecting on certain features presented by the objects of sense-perception and Understanding, and we are reflecting at the level of Understanding. That is to say we are doing our best to interpret the deliverance of sense and Understanding in the light of Understanding, but we are not interpreting sense-perception and Understanding from a philosophic level. We record, abstract, and classify; we do not criticize and construct. Our results—our classes of predicable qualities, our types of symbolizable relations, or the forms of judgement and inference which we detect— have the indifferent self-subsistence which the Understanding accords to all its objects, and they are, until we criticize the Understanding itself, inviolable in their isolation.

2·2. Empirical predicates, then, are all more or less sensuous. No doubt in empirical judgement we are in some sense thinking, and the predicate is consequently in some sense universal. But this thinking is not very much more than sense-perception and imagination (*Vorstellung*). The predicate has application at most to a class of *sensibilia*, or in the case of mathematical predicates we might say *quasi-sensibilia*. No doubt it is universal inasmuch as any class of *sensibilia* is an indefinite multiplicity admitting of limitation only in fact and not in principle. But this universality, like the uniqueness of the subject in a singular empirical judgement, is conferred upon it very largely by the nature of the act of sense-perception.[1]

3. There is another type of predicate to be discovered in the thinking of the Understanding. If we say (a) '*x* is sub-

[1] Cf. ch. iv, § 4·2 above.

stance', or (b) 'x exemplifies cause and effect', then the predicate is universal in a deeper sense. For *any* thing of common experience is (a) a substance in a certain state; and (b) its state is determined by a cause, and it determines causally the state of other substances. This type of predicate is all-pervasive within the ambitus of the Understanding's object-world, and although it is predicated of sensible things, it does not characterize them *qua* sensible but *qua* intelligible. It is a thought and not a sense-image. Even in predominantly sensuous experience the universal is present not simply as a particular quality or quantity ('red', e.g., or 'a foot high') which attaches to this or that indefinite multiplicity, but also as quality in general, or quantity in general, which no sense-content can lack: there is the germ of thought in sense, though there is not judgement save so far as the Understanding is active in reconstituting the sense-world as itself.

3·1. There is a further point of difference. Empirical predicates do not in themselves show any necessary connexion with one another. We are accustomed to use them every day with an implied context of systematic connexion; but that is to say we do not, and could not, ever experience solely those contents which with reference to judgement we call empirical predicates. For the second type of predicate is always in fact operative by implication in our experience. Empirical predicates taken by themselves—so far as that abstraction is possible—could not be said even to be 'juxtaposed' or 'separated': even so much order would annul the abstraction. Their multiplicity is as indefinite as that of the *sensibilia* which they classify. By themselves they would present a brute chaos, and for any sort of connexion and differentiation predicates of the second type are indispensable. Moreover, predicates of the second type not only enable us to order and connect the world we experience; they also, as we shall see, connect in an ordered way with one another.

This second type of predicate begins to reveal the nature of the Hegelian *Denkbestimmung* or category.

3·2. In this rough sketch I have simply assumed with common sense that judgement attributes a predicate to a thing called a subject, and within predicates I have not distinguished between characters and relations.

As regards the second point it may perhaps help the reader if I suggest that the common modern doctrine that there are purely external relations is reached by first, after the manner of Hume, surreptitiously inserting into what are proclaimed to be simply given qualities much that is in fact relational, and by then according to these doctored empirical qualities just so much independence of relations as seems convenient. As a description of a certain level of thinking, given from the point of view of the thinker, this type of theory has a certain truth. But it belongs to the natural history of thought and not to the philosophic interpretation which any idealist logic must claim to offer. The philosophic interpretation of any level of thinking must transcend the point of view of the thinker who is at that particular level. No idealist logic can accept as finally true that measure of mutual independence in the variation of quality and relation which is of course never wholly absent from our ordinary thinking.

The first point raises a problem to which the whole logic of Hegel is one solution among many, and the answer cannot therefore be hurried. But a glance at the Kantian philosophy may help us to modify the crude *prima facie* view of judgement which belongs to common sense.

4. Cause and effect, the second instance of the more genuinely universal predicate which I took in § 3, is numbered among the Kantian categories,[1] and Kant's conception of a category throws much light upon such predicates. A category, as Kant sees it, is not a mere predicate of a *de facto* presented object-world; it is also, *qua* a form of judgement, a function of the mind; it is a way of understanding as well as a character of what is understood. It characterizes, as its function, a spontaneously active intelligence as well as the phenomenal world which is the object and content of that intelligence. This seeming union of subjective and objective

---

[1] Cause and effect is in fact to Kant a schematized category: it is the pure category of ground and consequent as operative in our experience of a spatio-temporal world; see § 5·21 below. This distinction does not, however, immediately affect what follows.

in the Kantian category is a vitally important stage on the way to Hegel's Logic, but we must treat it with caution. Kant's position is far from unambiguous.[1] I must confess beforehand that I can say nothing of it without an amount of technical detail which some readers will find tedious, and that I am yet bound to treat it with a brevity which to others will appear far too simple and far too dogmatic. I shall try to explain it as Hegel sees it, though not in his precise words.

4·1. The categories (regarded as predicates) are not conceived by Kant as merely applying to any and every object experienced in the phenomenal world. They are all principles which characterize the phenomenal world as a whole. That, e.g., the law of cause and effect, as a law of external determining, holds everywhere in the phenomenal world[2] is an index of that world's *phenomenal* character. Doubtless it is also an index of the fact that the phenomenal world does not constitute a genuine, i.e. a self-conditioning, whole. Indeed, it is just this failure to be a genuine whole, just this instability displaying itself in indefinite regress, in which that world's phenomenality consists. Nevertheless, the Kantian categories characterize the phenomenal world *qua* phenomenal. They do therefore each partially define it, if not as a whole at least in respect to its claim to wholeness. They are in short more truly universal than empirical predicates, not merely because they characterize any and every phenomenal object but also because they each partially define the phenomenal world as at any rate a *quasi*-whole.

4·11. The student of Kant may perhaps object that the category of reciprocity is definitely said by Kant to systematize phenomena as a *Weltganzes*.[3] Doubtless this implies that any phenomenal object is known as in principle connected reciprocally with all other phenomena, but it is to be remembered that these other phenomena constitute a world

---

[1] e.g. the categories of modality do not seem to possess this dual aspect; see below, § 4·311.

[2] Or, if we think of the subjective aspect of a category, in every act of judgement in which the world of possible experience is actualized.

[3] KRV, B, p. 265, footnote. No doubt Kant holds that an Idea of Reason operates when we think phenomena as a *Weltganzes* (cf. KRV, B, p. 434), but it operates only regulatively and not constitutively; cf. § 4·4 below.

of merely possible experience.[1]   It is therefore hard to dispute Schopenhauer's contention that Kant's dynamical communion of all substances through their accidents is no more than the causal relation working two ways at once. If it is not, Kant is virtually admitting a concept of the unconditioned, or self-conditioned, as constitutive. In the *Critique of Judgment* Kant seems to feel the difficulty of confining human knowledge to this 'world-whole' which has no higher constitutive principle to unify it than the transcendental unity of apperception expressed through the category of reciprocity. There the teleological judgement is said to be reflective and not determinant, regulative and not constitutive:[2] 'The *transcendental* concept of purpose in Nature is neither a concept of Nature nor of freedom, for it attributes nothing to Nature as an object.' Yet it does (though 'merely') 'represent the way in which we *must necessarily* proceed in *reflecting on* natural objects, *with a view to a thoroughly connected experience.*'[3]

4·2. To say that the Kantian category is a universal which characterizes the phenomenal world as a whole, or *quasi*-whole, is to say that it is necessary as well as general. And this necessity is *a priori*, or pure; i.e. it is bound up with and guaranteed by the function of the intelligence (Understanding). It is a necessity at once of fact and act: that phenomenal objects must be, e.g., causally connected, and that we must think them as causally connected, are two sides of one truth, which can also be put by saying that the category is at once a structural character of the phenomenal world and a necessary form of all possible experience. Hence the guarantee of universality and necessity[4]—the assurance that the world has structural characters which belong to it as a whole and must belong to it—rests on an identity of nature

---

[1] See next section.

[2] So far like the Ideas of Reason; cf. § 4·4 below.

[3] *Critique of Judgment*, Introduction, p. xxxiv; italics mine. Kant's argument is that the categories are in a sense exhibited in sensuous presentation: although one does not 'see' cause and effect, yet one sees what without that category could not enter into our experience of an object, and so could not really be perceived at all. But the purposiveness of an organism does nothing to make possible the perceiving of it.

[4] Terms which are in effect synonymous for Kant.

in the intelligence and the object-world. It is the transcendental unity of apperception,[1] the unity of the Understanding *qua* appercipient subject in all possible experience, which makes the phenomenal world a whole, or *quasi*-whole; and this unity, objective because it is subjective,[1] is specialized in the categories, which further explicate this dual aspect, being at once functions of the Understanding's spontaneous activity (which is judgement) and *ipso facto* definitory characters of the phenomenal world.

Thus the mere generality of the empirical predicate gives place to a universal which characterizes some sort of whole, and characterizes necessarily because it is a phase in the unifying activity of a subject.

4·21. It is here worth while pausing to recall that the Greek for 'universal' is καθόλου, which means 'predicated of a whole' (not of a class or aggregate), and that Aristotle had both insisted that necessity is the distinctive character of the universal,[2] and asserted the identity of subject and object to be explicit in actual knowledge and implicit even in sense-perception. But Aristotle nowhere openly connects these two doctrines. Yet if the indefinite multiplicity of things depends on matter and only exists for sense-perception, then we verge on the conclusion that thought, if it really is thought, can only have for its object the world as a whole; that thought moves in universals because its object is always, at any rate implicitly, the universe.

4·3. We must now consider a little the limitations of the Kantian category.

Enough has already been said to make it clear that Kant's unity of the Understanding, appercipient in its object-world, is not the unity of a fully self-subsistent reality. On his view the categories define only the phenomenal world, and define it only as a *quasi*-whole: they have no application to the unconditioned (i.e. self-conditioned) thing-in-itself. Accordingly they are only forms of *possible* experience, valid rather than real, empty unless what Kant calls a 'corresponding' sense-intuition gives them content. Thus Kant, not venturing to assert save in one passage problematically that

[1] See above, ch. vii, § 5.
[2] Cf., e.g., *Posterior Analytics*, i, ch. iv.

sense and Understanding have a common stem, makes them co-operant on somewhat obscure terms in the activity of knowing an object. On the one hand, sense provides the matter, Understanding the form, of experience,[1] and so far sense would seem to be its proximate lower self which the Understanding reconstitutes. On the other hand, their community of source is quite problematic—we cannot possibly know it—and usually Kant assigns them a more or less co-ordinate importance in the knowing of an object, or even awards the palm to sense. Accordingly Kant's categories considered in themselves are merely valid, or 'prescriptive'. We may call them structural characters of the phenomenal world, and it is true that he entitles one of them 'substance and accident', a phrase hard to rid of very different historical associations. It is further true that they are all special forms of the unity of apperception and compel us to assume that all phenomenal objects belong to one *Weltganzes*, and that no object, however directly experienced, can be known save as constituted through them. Nevertheless Kant's phenomenal world is not actual and concrete save in the knowing of this or that finite subject when he is judging this or that instance of, for example, cause and effect.

4.31. Thus the Kantian category has a somewhat obscure dual nature. (A) Actual knowing remains for Kant still largely dominated by that aspect of indefinite multiplicity radiating out from a focus of 'this here and now', which is characteristic of sense-perception. So far the categories are principles valid *a priori* for any object which any singular subject may come to experience. In actually knowing a par-

---

[1] This of course is to over-simplify. In space and time, the *a priori* forms, which are also *a priori* contents, of our sensuous intuition, sense has its own element of form, to which a manifold of passively received sensation relates as matter. I have also ignored the imagination, which appears as mediating between the human faculties of sense and Understanding so soon as we consider not the logical but the psychological aspect of experience; i.e. so soon as we pass from (*a*) showing that the pure categories must be valid if any being whose thinking is discursive and requires complementation by non-intellectual intuition is to have objective knowledge, to (*b*) showing how in the special case of human spatio-temporal experience the categories operate schematized. This is the significance of Kant's distinction between (*a*) the objective, and (*b*) the subjective sides of his transcendental deduction of the categories.

ticular object as, e.g., a case of cause and effect, such a singular experient *knows* it as a particular pair of terms in what he *thinks* as an indefinite series of terms, each one of which is Janus-faced, its successor's cause and its predecessor's effect. The categories are universal and necessary, but this is not because they characterize a world independent of being the object of experience; it is because they are the forms of any singular subject's possible experience. They must be conceived, so to say, as radii whose centre is the singular subject's actual experience, and so merely as valid.

This may suggest a relapse upon Hume's naturalistic explanation of necessity in terms of a *de facto* purely subjective habit of connecting. But Kant was well aware that judgement entails in the judging subject the assertion that the truth of what he judges true is not simply dependent on his own or any other singular subject's judging. Hence (B) although all phenomena as a *Weltganzes* are never a total actual object of experience to the singular experient— although the radii, so to say, terminate at no definite circumference—yet Kant cannot dispense with a complementary notion of his categories as structural characters of a world which, though phenomenal, is one for all experients.

But here an obvious difficulty arises. A finite experient can only recognize the world of his own experience as a unitary world common for all experients in so far as he recognizes himself as, *qua* experient, universal. So much Kant himself admits in according to the singular experient a general awareness that he is active intelligence, an awareness given in the unity of apperception. But such a merely general awareness is quite inadequate ground for the recognition of a world common to all experients. If a finite experient could not recognize his own experience as together with the experience of other men in some measure concretely differentiating and not merely repeating a common world of possible experience, he could recognize no common world at all. Awareness, that is to say, of a world common to all experients belongs to finite minds only if they are differentiations of a universal mind. But the critical philosophy remains in a half-way position. It is far from being Kant's purpose to attribute our experience of necessity

to a peculiarity of men's minds which has to be taken
naturalistically as bare fact, but he will not conceive mind
as concretely universal.

4·311. Nowhere is this reluctance more obvious than in
Kant's treatment of the modal categories. The first nine
categories are structural characters of the *quasi*-whole
phenomenal world as well as functions of judgement, but the
modal categories express nothing beyond variation in the
singular experient's attitude towards an object which does
not vary concomitantly in content. The order in which Kant
sets out the modal categories is not logical but merely
psychological. The singular experient is conceived as passing from knowledge of one and the same constant object as
possible, to knowledge of it as actual, and thence to knowledge of it as necessary. Kant's previous nine categories have
progressively determined any possible object as extensive
quantum, as intensive quantum, as substance and accident,
as cause and effect, and finally as interaction of substances
through their accidents. But in treating the modal categories Kant in effect abandons the aspect of a category as
structural character. He beats a retreat, and, consciously or
not, conceives knowing only in terms of the singular experient. He is therefore unable to offer any explanation as
to how possibility can be one among a set of categories which
are, one and all, forms of possible experience. His position
here seems to be precisely that which any realist who is not
prepared to allow a real contingency in things must adopt
towards the problem of possibility:[1] If there be no contingency *in re*, then the difference between possible, actual, and
necessary can only express either different degrees or amounts
of knowledge, or some sort of difference between opinion
and knowledge: it is purely subjective variation in the face
of an objective thing which in itself is at once actual and
necessary—and, if it be worth adding, possible. The realist
effort to explain how on such a position the judgement (or
opinion?) that A is possibly or probably B can be true has
not met with conspicuous success, but here the point is that
for the critical philosophy the object is not thing-in-itself.
Yet if it is not, Kant's doctrine of modality is ruined. Because

---

[1] And/or of probability.

he denies to the modal categories an objective, structural aspect, his doctrine twists to realism in his hands.[1] Although his treatment of the first nine categories suggests a more frankly idealist solution of the dilemma which possibility presents to realism, yet Kant is blind to it. It was left for Hegel to show in the logic of Essence that our experience of possible, actual, and necessary in the phenomenal world depends upon contrast just as much as does our experience of cause and effect, and that the former experience is no less a determining of the structure of the phenomenal object than is the latter.[2]

Thus the modal categories in Kant offer a peculiar difficulty; but all Kant's categories still bear strong traces of that indefinite multiplicity which distinctively characterizes the object-world of sense-perception. The category of cause and effect is a principle of mechanical *ab extra* determining: its necessity reveals an obverse of contingency, and it turns out after all to be a universal not developed so very far beyond the persistent or self-repetitive universal of sense-perception, the empirical concept which in judgement is the abstract general predicate.

4.32. At the risk of seeming prolix I must pursue further this ambiguity in the Kantian category.

In the Introduction to KRV Kant, using the terms synthesis and analysis only with reference to concepts, draws a dubious distinction between synthetic judgements which expand knowledge and analytic judgements which merely clarify it. If the predicate is contained in the concept of the subject, the judgement is analytic; if it is not, the judgement

[1] It must also involve him—as it ultimately involves realism—in the Cartesian view that the mind can entertain a 'floating' idea without judging (cf. ch. xiii, § 4.3). For if the content of an idea remains constant while the mind's attitude to the independently real object varies, then the idea has as independent, as self-subsistent a being as the object. This comes out clearly in Hegel's criticism of Kant's attack on the ontological argument for God's existence; see LL, ii, pp. 172–6, and EL, § 193.

[2] Kant himself had felt that there must be some significance in the fact that all the dynamical categories, modal as well as relational, present themselves as pairs of correlates. It must, he says, have a ground in the nature of the Understanding. But this remark occurs only in the second edition (KRV, B, p. 110)

is synthetic, and is only valid if intuition accompanies it. But Kant also holds that all judgement which yields knowledge of an object is both synthetic and analytic, since it entails both synthesis and analysis of *intuitions*.[1] This second doctrine we have now to examine.

Kant gives the name of analysis to what he regards as one factor in all cognitive judgement, viz. a comparing of intuitions, and, through abstraction from all their differences, an eliciting of general concepts, or marks. Concepts thus elicited are analytic, not synthetic, universals,[2] and, irrespective of their particular content, they are united (e.g. as subjects and predicates) in judgement[3] according to certain unvarying formal relations. These formal relations are the traditional forms of judgement elaborated by formal logic, which Kant believes to have performed its task to perfection. This analysis of intuitions was mistaken by Locke for the full nature of judgement; and Locke—somewhat inconsistently with his view of these intuitions as simple ideas, self-evident and self-contained atoms—believed all our serious knowledge to result from subsequent comparison of these general concepts, or 'abstract ideas'.[4] In effect he regarded thinking as in its full nature no more than what, on Kant's view, is a part of that temporal process which our own mind presents to each of us in so far as we know it—and we know it no further—through inner sense as phenomenal object. Locke's 'plain historical method' was thus an attempt to retain the attitude of the ordinary empirical thinker, and he failed to observe that this abstractive analysis of general concepts presupposes data far other than the atomically simple ideas which he himself posits: it presupposes data which are themselves products of the synthesis of general concepts. However simple-seeming the intuitions we analyse—be they no more than patches of a uniform colour—yet each is

[1] Professor Paton in *Kant's Metaphysic of Experience* seems to establish this beyond doubt.

[2] i.e. abstract) (concrete universals, as are *all* the concepts of our Understanding. The synthetic or concrete universal could only belong to an intuitive intellect; see *Critique of Judgment*, pp. 348–9.

[3] Hence all cognitive judgement is in fact synthesis of concepts as well as of intuitions.

[4] A procedure still analytic in Kant's sense of the term.

already constituted and known only through a general concept, and none is so simple but that several concepts have gone to constitute it.

Moreover, this presupposition of synthesis by analysis is not any temporal priority. No doubt so long as we view our empirical experience empirically it appears to us a temporal alternation of analysis and synthesis, but to the critical philosopher time is a formal factor in empirical experience, not the unquestionable presupposition of his own critical reflection. Analysis presupposes synthesis not temporally but logically, and from the critical standpoint the two are inseparable factors in all judgement. The only element in knowing which can be called sheer datum is not simple atomic ideas but a sensuous manifold of which as such we are not conscious. It is but the formless residue after abstraction not only from judgement and the forms of concepts but also from space and time, which, too, are *a priori*.[1]

4·33. Yet this manifold is passively received. The 'agent' or 'donor' is the unknown thing-in-itself, not Locke's naïvely conceived real body so constituted as directly to reproduce itself in our ideas of primary qualities and indirectly to produce our ideas of secondary qualities. Nevertheless the passivity of sensation and the fact that our intuition, despite its *a priori* nature, lacks activity betray an obvious relic of realism in Kant's view.[2] No doubt for Kant intuition without concepts is blind; no doubt the universality and necessity which the Understanding contributes *a priori* are a condition of objective knowing; yet thought does not on Kant's view constitute the object in respect of its reality.

[1] See footnote on § 4·3 above.

[2] Kant calls both intuition and sensibility 'passive' in contrast with the active Understanding; thus emphasizing the break between sense and thought which, in order to mediate between Locke and Leibniz, he deliberately and consistently maintains. But in point of fact sensibility, as he describes it, *reacts* to the 'influence' of the thing-in-itself, which it passively receives. It modifies it in reproducing it as an empirical manifold for the *a priori* forms of our intuition to inform. Indeed, if it did not, things-in-themselves would possess all the sensuous qualities. Sensibility is therefore not after all wholly passive. And since intuition has *a priori* forms, it is hard to avoid the conclusion that it possesses a degree of activity greater than sensibility and less than Understanding. Kant was far behind Aristotle in his insight into the essential connexion between activity and form.

Our Understanding is wholly discursive; although it is active, yet it is non-intuitive, emphatically not creative of its own object;[1] it is dependent on the gift of sense for the moment of immediacy and individuality. Hence Kant seems on the whole to think that the subject's immediate contact in sense with reality is that which sets the seal of objectivity on the content of experience and makes possible true judgement about the empirically real; to believe that from sense and not from thought comes, so to say, that spark of life which enables *a priori* judgements to be synthetic, in the sense of expansive and not merely clarificatory, and yet valid of objects. Because 'Man's Reason is in such deep insolvency to sense', because it cannot be shown that sense is actualized, or reconstituted, without residue in the thinking of the Understanding, Kant wavers towards reversing the functions of sense and thought and maintaining that the actualization of the universal concept in sense-intuition is all that knowing is.[2] Although all judgement is both analytic and synthetic, and although the object is phenomenal and not known save as necessarily connected within the one phenomenal world, yet this analysis and synthesis is not any self-development of the object in judgement. Any suggestion that we reason by implication because our object is a self-transcending finite whose nature lies always beyond it is quite alien to Kantian doctrine.

4·34. For these reasons—or, to sum them up shortly, because thought, though always both synthetic and analytic, is purely discursive and non-intuitive—Kant inevitably tends towards viewing the concept as an abstract universal, and judgement as subsumptive.[3] If thought is quite un-

---

[1] See, e.g., KRV, B, pp. 138–9.

[2] Compare a trace of similar empiricism in Aristotle, *Prior Analytics*, ii, ch. 21. See also below on Bradley, ch. xiii, § 4·7.

[3] Cf. KRV, B, p. 171. In the chapter on schematism in KRV Kant calls the schema a universal rule of synthesis, but he still describes judgement as subsuming an image under the schema, as if the latter were a mere abstract class-concept.

In Kant's transcendental logic the centre of interest is judgement. Had Kant paid more attention to the nature of inference he might have found it less easy to deny to thought its native moment of intuition. The discursive factor in thought is not revealed only in the dispersion of an identical concept

intuitive there can be no concrete universal, no concept which *in itself* is unity in difference; which *qua* thought is both form and content. On Kant's view the Understanding actively synthesizes concepts, and through concepts sense-intuitions; but Kant's concepts in themselves and apart from a sense-given matter are purely formal, not self-particularizing. Furthermore, as they are in themselves bare identities, so they are, for anything that Kant can show, without any essential communion with one another. It is only in the particular intuited object that they are in synthetic union. That is their only meeting-point; outside it they are unconnected valid forms. This is equally true of all Kant's concepts. The pure concept, the category, is an active function of synthesis as well as a concept, but it is as empty of native content, as innocent of self-differentiation, as the empirical concepts which in the first instance it synthesizes. Again, the transcendental unity of apperception is somehow specialized in the categories, but this is no concrete unity in difference.[1] Kant is convinced that formal logic, by successfully

through a multiplicity of sensuous intuitions which instantiate it, but also in the movement of inference from premisses to conclusion; and in the grasping of a conclusion a complementary factor of intellectual intuition is plainly manifest, not as an act separate from discursion but as the re-immediation of the discursive, mediatory movement. But this is concealed from Kant by his view of the relation of syllogism to Reason. He holds that Reason relates to syllogism as Understanding relates to judgement. An Idea of Reason (in general) is the concept of the totality of conditions (and therefore the concept of the unconditioned) as containing a ground for the synthesis of the conditioned (KRV, B, p. 379). In other words, it is the thought of a completed whole of all the prosyllogisms required to justify a conclusion. Whereas Aristotle had insisted that, if demonstration was to be possible at all, an actual intuition by νοῦς of absolutely primary premisses must limit the regress of prosyllogisms, Kant confines the role of Reason to a merely regulative thinking. Thus up to a point Kant follows the Aristotelian tradition of regarding inference as linear, and he accepts the corollary, so forcibly disputed by Aristotle, that the premisses of inference must regress indefinitely. From this he concludes that the completion of the regressive series is a merely regulative Idea. And although he advances beyond the linear and towards the systematic conception of inference in that he regards this completion as an ideal totality of all the conditioning premisses and not as a self-evident primary premiss, nevertheless he conceives this Idea of totality—and, accordingly, the conclusion of any given syllogism—as wholly unintuitive.

[1] For some hint of a different view in Kant see § 5·11 below.

eliciting all the formal relations in which concepts *qua* united in judgement can stand to one another, has shown that the Understanding in itself is a system, and has thereby provided him with a backdoor entrance to the categories and relieved him from any need of showing how they cohere systematically. But he cannot tell us how formal logic was able to discover and exhibit this systematic connexion. And that is scarcely surprising. For if Understanding without sense is utterly empty, it is meaningless to call it a system at all.[1] Kant's teaching that time and space are *a priori* both as forms and as contents shows far more insight than his doctrine of a purely discursive thought. The principle of matter and form pervades Kant's whole theory of knowledge, but he had far less perception of its exigencies than Aristotle.[2]

4·4. Man's speculative Reason is held by Kant to be a higher faculty than his Understanding. Yet Kant exhibits it as yet emptier than Understanding. For it does not provide a higher phase of form to which sense and Understanding together relate as proximate matter.

Kant, officially at any rate, restricts knowledge to an awareness of the phenomenal world revealed through the co-operation of sense with the unifying activity of the Understanding specialized in the categories. The unconditioned thing-in-itself, which the notion of a phenomenon necessarily implies, can be *thought* by Reason, and this rational thinking plays a vitally important regulative function in our experience, confining our Understanding to its proper object. But Reason, though it *thinks* the unconditioned, does not *know* it. The Ideas of Reason, on Kant's view, constitute no object—as the categories of the Understanding constitute the phenomenal object—because man has no intellectual intuition.

5. Hegel's conception of a category is at once a criticism and a development of Kant's, but to begin with I will merely contrast their two views, expressing Kant's position

---

[1] Mr. Joseph is, I think, making the same criticism of Kant when he charges him with confusing the antithesis of universal and particular with the antithesis of intelligible and sensible; see *Essays in Ancient and Modern Philosophy*, ch. x, especially pp. 273 ff.

[2] Cf. footnote 2 on p. 95.

in a manner which I hope will complement what I have already said.

The Kantian category is a form of possible experience, a valid rule which every cognitive act of a finite thinker must actualize. The phenomenal world of which this category is all-pervasive has its being only as an object which in respect of its form is constituted by the mind. But Kant, despite the anticipatory interpretations of the Critique offered by some of his nineteenth-century commentators, does not by mind mean a universal mind: he means no more than any and every finite mind, so natured as to inform a sense-given matter in a certain way and thereby to know phenomenal objects. Accordingly the notion of a finite mind essentially self-transcending in all its activities is not dreamt of in his philosophy. Indeed, such a notion is meaningless unless the object is taken as self-transcending in judgement, and we have seen that this is not Kant's teaching. Kant's limitation of self-consciousness, too, quite obviously precludes it; for on his view each of us knows his individual self as a merely phenomenal object which changes in time. It is true that Kant holds the phenomenal self and the phenomenal not-self—the 'outer' world—to be possible objects of consciousness only in and through their mutual contrast. It is also true that on his view they are—at least in all cognitive awareness—identical in content with one another in a sense which is vital to Kant's proof that we have objectively valid knowledge,[1] although not in a sense which is easy for Kant to make precise. Nevertheless this empirical self which we know is in no sense at all known as subject, and incidentally the consequences for Kant's moral philosophy are disastrous. Beyond this consciousness of an empirical self our self-consciousness is limited by Kant to our bare recognition of the purely general nature of the subject as an active intelligence. It is most plausibly suggested by Professor Paton that Kant, under the influence of Leibniz, still conceived the

[1] This becomes quite obvious in the proof of the Second Analogy, and it follows directly from the fact that both self and not-self are phenomenal: Kant's doctrine of phenomena is idealist and not realist. It is also obvious from the fact that according to Kant time is the immediate condition of inner phenomena and thereby the mediate condition of outer phenomena.

individual mind as a monad;[1] not a windowless monad, since it informs a given which it receives,[2] but still not anything in its own nature self-transcending. In the place of any doctrine of self-transcendence there stand in Kant's philosophy only (a) his recognition that phenomenon implies noumenon, i.e. that the thing which is known as it appears must be at least thinkable as being in itself; and (b) his appeal to the thing-in-itself as the source which influences our passive sensibility to provide the *a priori* forms of intuition and Understanding with a brute matter of sensation, an appeal which smacks of realism and raises the question whether, for all that Kant can show, the empirical manifold may not be quite alien to those *a priori* forms in whose embrace it must acquiesce.

Hegel, on the other hand, finds in the commonest experience of self-consciousness a clear revelation of self-transcendence,[3] and he does not hesitate to seize its implication. The finite individual mind can only be self-transcending if universal mind is immanent in it; only if its activity is that in which spirit does and must express itself.[4] Hence for Hegel thought is intuitive as well as discursive; not form without content of its own, but concrete universal. An Hegelian category is therefore not a mere necessary rule for possible experience, not a subjective form merely valid because *we* must impose it. If our minds in a measure constitute their object, it is so only because *they* are constituted by the activity of universal spirit in them. Therefore a category is valid for any finite thinker's possible experience only because it is a self-definition of spirit, a phase of spirit which *is* the activity of constituting itself in constituting finite minds.

5·1. Hegel's criticism of Kant is best approached through his attacks on the Kantian Ideas of Reason.

---

[1] *Kant's Metaphysic of Experience*, i, p. 183.

[2] i.e. Leibniz's monad is so utterly self-enclosed an individual that he must explain away sense as confused thought. But for Kant a being which sensates is a being which is affected from without.

[3] Cf. ch. viii, § 3·11 above.

[4] Cf. § 1·2 above. That to Kant any such view is totally alien is perhaps most obvious in his repeated statements that if the objects which we know were things-in-themselves our knowledge of them would be *a priori*.

We have seen that for Hegel thought is never devoid of intuition. He points out that Kant's sharp distinction of knowing from thinking is in the last resort nonsensical. To know the limited is to make a significant negative judgement, and therefore entails knowledge of what it is which limits. Hence to know the phenomenal world as conditioned is *eo ipso* to know the unconditioned. The distinction of thing-in-itself from phenomenon must fall within our objective experience. If it does not, there is no better ground for believing that the Ideas regulate our empirical experience than that they yield knowledge of the thing-in-itself. Either belief might be due to subjective habit, and neither need even be common to the whole human race. In short, the rational Ideas of the unconditioned are regulative, not in the sense that they merely restrict the Understanding while encouraging it to extend its knowledge at its own level, but because they are operative and constitutive *in* the knowledge even of the Understanding.[1]

Because Kant severs Understanding from sense-intuition below and Reason above, Hegel holds him ultimately a subjective idealist. Kant had the great merit in Hegel's eyes of

[1] The Kantian scholar may object that Kant conceives the Idea not only as negatively regulative but also as a norm, as the thought of an unconditioned totality to which we must think the object we know as in some sense approximating. But in precisely what sense? Kant does not and cannot make this clear, because he rigidly divorces the normative from the constitutive function of thought. The ideal as Kant opposes it to the real becomes inevitably the unreal and empty. In all his works Kant exalts the importance of Ideas; often he seems on the very verge of allowing them a constitutive function. But the residue of realism in his philosophy forbids categorically any such admission. On the view to which he is committed from the start of his critical thinking, sense must be treated as a source of knowledge separate from thought, and experience is not self-transcending. The world we know is only phenomenal, only empirically real; but in that world there are no degrees of reality, and, correspondingly, no degrees of truth. Hence Kant cannot possibly treat the thought of anything beyond mechanically behaving phenomena as more than *mere* thought which is not knowledge. That his weaker followers should abandon the thing-in-itself and sink into sheer phenomenalism was as natural as that occasionalism should result from the dualist theory of Descartes. Hegel's idealism and sheer phenomenalism are in fact the two alternatives to which Kant's fundamentally unstable position must give rise. We shall consider in ch. xiv Hegel's effort to reunite the normative and constitutive functions of thought.

making self-consciousness central in his system, but he failed
to expand the bare formula 'I am I', the mere certainty of
Reason that it is all reality,[1] into a self-conscious totality
of spirit. Even his specializing of the transcendental unity
of apperception in the categories was not a genuine articulation of it, but a filling borrowed uncritically from the forms
of judgement elaborated by formal logic. Hegel calls it 'an
insult to science', and 'where', he adds, 'shall Understanding
be able to exhibit necessity, if it cannot show it in its own
self, which *is* pure necessity?'[2] His point is that Kant offers
no basis for his categories but empirical distinctions; distinctions which belong to the natural history of thought,
however true it be that in the reflection of the formal logicians who elicited them there was the evident germ of
Reason.[3] Kant does not feel the need to exhibit the necessary
mutual connexion of the categories of the Understanding,
because he has not himself effectively transcended the level
of the Understanding. But he has thereby virtually confessed that he cannot show how his own whole critical
inquiry is possible. Indeed its possibility is logically precluded by the restriction of knowledge to phenomena, and
Kant's immense achievement rests upon a radical incon-
sistency. For there can be no purely immanent metaphysics.
The official critical philosophy suffers the fate of all phenomenalism. Taken as it stands, the *Critique of Pure Reason* is
an inevitably self-defeating attempt to philosophize while
remaining at the level of the Understanding, a sacrifice of
philosophy upon the altar of natural science and mathematics.

5·11. This criticism is so important that we may pause to

---

[1] See *Phän*. JE ii, pp. 185–6.

[2] Ibid. In EL, §§ 40–60, Hegel presents a masterly general criticism of
Kant's philosophy. His attitude to Kant is already well developed in *Glauben
und Wissen* (1802). In discussing Kant, as in treating other predecessors of
Hegel, I have often tried to develop Hegel's general attitude to them in more
detail than he does himself.

[3] Hegel, of course, does not mean that the judgement-forms of formal logic
are merely mythical. He reproduces them all, reinterpreted, in his own categories of Judgement. He means that neither the formal logicians nor Kant
have explained their number, interrelation, or order, and that they have thus
failed to penetrate to their real nature.

consider it in more detail. Hegel may appear to do less than justice to Kant. In the first place it seems to be Kant's doctrine that all the forms of judgement—the various purely formal relations, i.e. in which formal logic has shown that concepts must stand to one another in judgement—are involved in any act of knowing. If so, it should follow that *all* the categories—the forms of thought in its complementary and equally universal synthetic aspect—are also operative in any particular act of judgement.[1] Secondly, Kant does note it as matter for reflection that the three subdivisions in each of his four main groups of categories are related 'moments' such that the two first combine to produce the third as a fresh thought,[2] a doctrine in which Hegel himself detects a prophecy of his own dialectical connexion of categories. Furthermore, in the Analytic of Principles Kant tries to prove each of the schematized categories to be necessarily presupposed and actually operative in our experience. His method seems to be to prove each Principle by showing that any and every judgement of experience would be impossible without it; but these proofs do show an unmistakable order of progression throughout. Nevertheless Hegel's main contention remains. Because Kant restricts knowledge to knowledge through the categories of the phenomenal world, he cannot deduce his categories philosophically. Kant does not doubt that the Understanding is a systematic whole, but he is not in possession of the real clue to its nature. The categories are, on Hegel's view, bound together as phases in a single activity which transcends finite thinking, although it is immanent in it and constitutive of it. But for Kant 'fehlt das geistige Band'; he can only in the Analytic of Principles take up each schematized category in turn, and try to show that without it our experience of objects would not be possible. So his 'deduction', even if it be taken as including the Analytic of Principles, is little more than

---

[1] Incidentally, if all the categories are operative in, e.g., every judgement of perception and every mathematical judgement, it becomes hard to deny that finite experience is self-transcending.

[2] This first appears in KRV, B, pp. 110–11, and as a casual observation. But in the *Critique of Judgment*, Introduction, footnote to p. lvii, Kant defends the essentially trichotomous character of philosophical division.

a posteriori derivation.[1] When the thing-in-itself is completely withdrawn from our knowledge, the *a priori* element
in experience, which Kant strove so strenuously to isolate,
tends to collapse into complete immanence. The distinction
between *a priori* and *a posteriori* almost disappears. It can in
fact only be retained by Kant at the cost of making sense a
source of knowledge independent of the purely discursive
Understanding.

5·12. This criticism is assuredly borne out if we examine
the very ambiguous account of philosophical knowledge
which Kant gives in the Discipline of Pure Reason.[2] All our
knowledge, he says, relates in the end to possible intuitions;[3]
but whereas mathematics constructs its concepts in an intuition which is *a priori* at once as form and as content, philosophy derives its knowledge from concepts, considering the
particular only in the universal.[4] Accordingly, philosophy
is the discursive use of Reason.[5] We have been told earlier
that 'Reason has for its object the Understanding only and
its fittest employment'.[6]

Thus Kant restricts the subject-matter of speculative
philosophy to the activity of the Understanding co-operant
with sense in the knowing of phenomenal objects. But the
term 'discursive' shows the difficulty he is in. Throughout
the KRV 'discursive' has been equivalent to 'non-intuitive'.
Kant cannot properly apply it to knowing, but only to thinking. For he has held throughout that (*a*) our thinking is
purely discursive, inasmuch as it is not in itself intuitive but
has to wait on sense-intuition for the moment of immediacy
and individuality, which knowing also entails; and that (*b*)
it is therefore not knowing.

Kant would presumably retort that philosophical knowledge does ultimately relate to possible intuitions. But that

---

[1] Kant means by *Deduktion* a justification of the categories, not, as Hegel
seems to assume, a proof of them as systematically entailing one another;
cf. Paton, op. cit. i, pp. 313–14. But that does not affect Hegel's main point.

[2] See KRV, B, pp. 740 ff. [3] Ibid., p. 747.

[4] Ibid., p. 742. Natural science is not here discussed because Kant is
mainly thinking of the efforts of rationalist philosophers to apply a mathematical method to philosophy. In natural science particular laws entail an
empirical element. [5] Ibid., p. 747.

[6] Ibid., p. 672.

is no defence. Sense-intuition can supply the moment of existence, or reality, only for the knowing of phenomenal objects, and experience as such—the co-operation of Understanding and sense-intuition in the knowing of phenomenal objects—cannot itself be a phenomenal object. Kant is raising the question: What *is* experience? What is the whole complex of mind cognizing its phenomenal object-world? And he is claiming some knowledge of the answer. He holds that this philosophical knowledge is not dogma, nor the fruit of demonstration, and it is his view that in philosophy definition is a goal and not an assumption. Yet the knowledge which he claims is knowledge. But knowledge which is not of empirical objects or mathematical constructions but knowledge of what experience *is*, must contain as an integral moment intuition which is not sensuous. If experience *is*, it *is* not as a phenomenal object *is*.[1] Every other sentence of the Critique of Pure Reason bears witness that the more modestly we try to limit the scope of human knowledge the more impossible it becomes to justify that knowledge which we do claim.

5.13. We may add what is both a complementary criticism of Kant and a corollary to Hegel's doctrine of self-consciousness and self-transcendence.

Kant sees in the passivity which is to him distinctive of sense the influence of the thing-in-itself, and by this irruption the continuity of the human spirit with Nature is brusquely severed. Kant has in fact no philosophy of Nature, only a philosophy of natural science. For him Nature, on this side of the thing-in-itself, exists only as the non-spiritual; i.e. as the outer phenomenal world of which natural science yields us the fullest truth we can have. He is thus driven to his obscure doctrine of double affection. He must hold that the material element in the phenomena of inner sense is due (*a*) ultimately to the influence of the thing-in-itself, but also (*b*) directly to the action of 'external' phenomena upon us. But (*b*), if it is true at all, is clearly a truth belonging to the standpoint of positive science. It may be a fact for physiology or empirical psychology; it certainly cannot fall within

---

[1] Professor Hoernlé states this difficulty admirably in a review of Professor Paton's 'Kant's Metaphysic of Experience' in *Mind*, October 1937, pp. 501–2.

the purview of critical philosophy, for it can obviously be known, if at all, only through the categories co-operating with intuition. Yet without it Kant can give no explanation of the special manner in which we are affected in inner as opposed to outer sense, of how inner sense is sense at all. He fails to see that the identity of content in inner and outer phenomena, demanded by his own proof of causality,[1] implies that no rigid barrier divides inner and outer consciousness, and that both must fall within self-consciousness in a wide meaning of the term. Denying self-transcendence, he misses the fact that sense at the immediate, undeveloped level at which it may be looked on as matter for thought to inform, is no less self-feeling than it is awareness of a not-self—or, rather, is the undivided germ of both.[2]

To Hegel, on the other hand, the relation of passive to active which emerges in sensuous experience implies no alien influence from without. It is an attitude of the mind to that lower phase of itself which the mind becomes aware of in its essentially self-reconstitutive development. The 'given' in sense is but its own lower self which the mind 'finds' confronting it; its seeming 'given' and alien character is an otherness which the mind has conferred upon itself.[3] In this manner Hegel carries down into a pre-spiritual Nature the serial phases of information which Kant abruptly terminates by introducing laterally, as it were, the influence of the unknown.

5·2. These criticisms of Kant may seem unduly to depreciate one of the world's half-dozen really great thinkers. Yet they will not if we remember that criticism is a moment of construction. To Hegel it seemed that no philosophy could be critical without being *ipso facto* reconstitutive of what it criticized,[4] and he never dreamt of minimizing that

---

[1] See § 5 above.

[2] In certain passages of the *Opus Postumum* Kant seems to suggest a self-in-itself which posits itself as object, and an empirical self which is not mere phenomenal object but synthetically active; cf. Kemp Smith, *Commentary on Kant's Critique of Pure Reason*, pp. 620–4. But it is hard to see how these hints are to be reconciled with critical views which Kant evidently still held. They betray dissatisfaction with inner sense, but not, I think, much inclination to a view such as Hegel's.   [3] Cf. ch. viii above, esp. §§ 3·1 and 3·11.

[4] In the preface to *Phän.* Hegel elaborates this thesis with great power.

positive aspect in the Critical Philosophy. In this spirit it
was that he set himself to fill in the two gaping chasms in the
Kantian universe. He strove in his Philosophies of Nature
and Spirit to exhibit an unbroken continuity holding together Nature, sense, Understanding, and Reason as phases
of a development that is ultimately the self-developing
activity which spirit is, and thus to disembarrass philosophy
of an ambiguous thing-in-itself which somehow emerges
from its unknowable isolation as the active source of our
passive sensibility, and thus severs sense from Nature. In
the Logic he attempted to express this total development in
the medium of pure thought, which, since it is the culminating phase of that development, must also, he believed, be
the truest form of it. Hence he accepts Kant's categories,
considerably modified and elaborated, as *Denkbestimmungen*,
and they appear transformed and absorbed in the first two
sections of his Logic, Being and Essence. They are only
the categories of the Understanding, *Denkbestimmungen* of
the finite phenomenal world; but that is still to say that, as the
philosopher must view them, they are self-definitions, though
partial and abstract self-definitions, of the Absolute[1] as finite
and phenomenal.[2] Kant, on the other hand, though he regarded them as essentially constitutive of an objective world,
was yet forced to hold them to be subjective (merely principles of *our* thinking), because that objective world of our
knowledge is merely phenomenal; because as an object of
knowledge it excludes absolutely, and is defined in stark
opposition to, the real but unknown noumenon.[3] Hegel's
Absolute also defines itself in categories which manifest the
universal as something far more than a valid principle of
mechanical determination, a necessity which is also contingency. Causation, for example, is not in Hegel's view only
knowable as a mutilated Aristotelian efficient cause shorn of

[1] = Absolute Spirit.

[2] It is thus important to observe that in Hegel the term 'Understanding'
means from one point of view a human faculty, a concrete attitude belonging
to Subjective Spirit (see ch. viii, §§ 2·3, 3·3, and 6), and from the other point
of view the activity of spirit so far as it is expressed in the categories of Being
and Essence. The term 'Reason' has a corresponding dual aspect.

[3] For the senses which the terms 'subjective' and 'objective' acquire in
Kant's philosophy see EL, § 41, *Zusatz* (2).

the other aspects of form, and teleology is neither a fairy tale nor a heuristic fiction. Nor are Kant's Ideas of Reason, properly interpreted, mere empty regulative thoughts. They contain in germ the highest categories of a truly philosophical logic.

5·21. In the foregoing comparison of Kant and Hegel I have almost ignored the distinction which Kant draws between the pure category and the category schematized to operate in experience of a spatio-temporal world. The reader may well be curious to know what is Hegel's attitude towards it, especially if he has observed that, to judge by their titles, Hegel's categories of Being and Essence would seem to include in one series both Kant's pure categories and his schematized categories as well as many other principles which Kant does not regard as categories at all.

The answer is not altogether easy. Here it must suffice to say that Hegel's categories as set forth in his Logic have no reference to space and time, which belong to the sphere of Nature. In this sense Hegel's categories are all pure categories. On the other hand, for Hegel thought does not lack the moment of intuition. He therefore cannot accept Kant's distinction as it stands. He does, however, find in Kant's schematized categories, when they are stripped of temporal reference, phases of thought which carry further and develop Kant's pure categories. For example, cause and effect, as we experience it, is a principle involving necessary succession in time. But Hegel considers that even as a pure category it is more than ground and consequent: it is a certain sort of productivity which the thought of ground and consequent merely prefigures.[1]

5·22. Secondly, I have only mentioned in a footnote[2] the distinction which Kant makes between the objective and subjective sides of his transcendental deduction of the categories. I believe this distinction, bound up as it is with Kant's doctrine of schematism, to have an important bearing on Hegel's distinction between logic and philosophy of spirit. But this is a difficult and intricate problem which we cannot here consider. Nevertheless it is vital to note one

[1] Kant also had regarded cause as productivity (as Hume had not).
[2] On § 4·3 above.

point in this connexion. Kant's objective deduction purports to be a purely logical proof that the transcendental unity of apperception, and therefore the categories, are indispensable for objective knowledge; it has no concern with the operation of a finite being's faculties in knowing. The Understanding is here considered as a system of truth-forms, not as a faculty;[1] there is no reference to space and time; the imagination is wholly ignored. Nevertheless the objective deduction *is* concerned with an *a priori* form of intuition,[2] though not a spatio-temporal form. Kant himself supposes that intuition so considered remains passive—even sensuous, though it is hard to give a meaning to sense without space and time. But surely it is harder still to see how an *a priori* intuition-form with which logic is concerned can fail to be an integral moment of thought. I think it is impossible in the last resort to reconcile Kant's procedure in his objective deduction with his view that thought is purely discursive.

5.23. Lastly, I must here pass over the relation in Kant of speculative to practical Reason, and of knowledge to religious faith. Kant's transcendental logic cannot be fully understood apart from his views on these problems, and Hegel's very different method of solving them is one of the reasons why his conception of logic seems so very far from Kant's. But these, too, are matters beyond our immediate scope.

6. We have seen that Hegel's categories connect with one another because they are phases in a single activity of spirit. In the following chapter we shall have to discuss the special nature of this interconnexion. Meanwhile it may be well to close the present chapter by reverting more or less to the common-sense level at which it opened, and making an attempt to compare Hegel's categories, considered simply as predicates or characters, with his forms of Nature and Concrete Spirit taken together.

Thus considered, the forms of Nature and Concrete Spirit will fall between empirical predicates and logical categories, and the three types can be roughly characterized as follows.

[1] Though still as activity. Cf. above, note 2, p. 107.
[2] And presumably also with an *a priori* content, a pure manifold of intuition; see note 1 on p. 90 above.

6·1. (1) Empirical predicates characterize only a limited subject. They have only a rudimentary universality, the mere generality which consists in qualifying an indefinitely repeated singular, and qualifying it *de facto* without exhibiting any necessary and universal connexion of it with its context. Accordingly they lack any real connexion among themselves. Finally—as all these defects indicate—they are still very largely sensuous.

6·11. (2) The forms of Nature and Concrete Spirit are thoughts, not sensuous images at all. They are not empirical predicates describing vaguely limited groups of things in a ready-made world of common sense or natural science. Each is universal, not in that rudimentary sense but because it pervades the whole world it characterizes at a certain level. Hegel, we have said, seeks the nature of the partially developed by asking first what it is for itself.[1] A phase of Concrete Spirit expresses the attitude of the subject to an object and content which is for it a total world; it does not describe *ab extra* a collection of minds experiencing each its own limited object. Some of the forms of Nature—vegetable and animal life, e.g.—might seem at first sight merely to characterize externally certain vaguely limited groups of individuals within a 'detached' world of non-spiritual Nature. But they do not: for the organism its environment is both *in pari materia* with it and all-comprehensive, just as for the conscious subject at any level its object and content is a total world. Life in Hegel's Philosophy of Nature is not a phenomenon juxtaposed to other phenomena of different kinds, not a patch in an alien context; it is, though not a fully adequate, yet an all-pervasive characterization of the world.[2]

The forms of Nature (which for philosophy is pre-spiritual and not non-spiritual) and the forms of Concrete

---

[1] See ch. vii, § 2·21, *ad fin.* above.

[2] Cf. ch. iii, §§ 5–5·4 above. I have there suggested that even the biological sciences cannot easily ignore this truth. Below organism this difficulty is at least less apparent, because approximation to subjectivity is still so distant. In space and time there is no difference between *für sich* and *für uns* (cf. ch. viii, § 4·3 above). In physical and chemical characterization the difference is but faintly prefigured: the world of Nature is here still so abstract that it scarcely suggests even the bastard, sensuous individuality of things collected in vaguely limited groups.

Spirit are not, like empirical predicates, devoid of real interconnexion. They are philosophical thoughts, and to the
philosopher they present themselves—so far resembling the
logical categories—as a developing series. Each term is
the more complete truth of its predecessor, and within the
series the culminating stage is immanent and operative.

Yet the forms of Nature and Concrete Spirit are thoughts
which still bear an obvious reference to sense. They are
forms which, like the specific forms of Aristotle, manifest
themselves in material embodiment even to the philosopher.
Even as he sees them, they gain expression in an existent
phenomenal world, which possesses a certain self-subsistence,
due, as it seems, to a residue in it of matter and contingency.
Hence the shape in which these forms present themselves
to the philosopher is in part determined by their reference
to sense, their aptness to phenomenal manifestation. They
are, on the other hand, thoughts, and they belong to the
content of philosophic thinking, which can and must discount phenomenal embodiment as an untrue form apper-
taining only to grades of spirit lower than itself. Philosophic
thinking is the conquest of contingency and finitude, and it
is itself partly moulded by the course of the struggle. But
the forms of Nature and Concrete Spirit do transcend the
apparent self-subsistence of the world in which they are
manifest. They express a criticism and a reconstitution of
that world.

I need scarcely add that these forms are not schematized
categories, not principles of a spatio-temporal order through
which the Understanding in common sense and natural
science thinks its 'detached' phenomenal objects. On the
contrary, Space and Time are Hegel's two first forms of
Nature, and the Understanding as a faculty—or, better, as
a concrete attitude of subject to object at a certain level of
experience—is a phase of Concrete Spirit.

6·12. (3) The categories are the pure thought which is
almost wholly latent in empirical experience, and still largely
latent in the Forms of Nature and Concrete Spirit, elements
though these are within the content of philosophic thinking.
The categories are the explicit definitions of the Absolute,
which the philosopher can claim to elicit only because

Absolute Spirit is immanent in his thinking. Ultimately they are for the same reason *self*-definitions of Absolute Spirit.

6·2. One might exemplify as follows the three types of universal. Minerals conceived as classes of physical things are empirical universals. Chemical combination, on the other hand, is a more or less intelligible form of identity in diversity. It is a thought, though it still has reference to matter: it is a form of Nature. But identity in diversity itself is a logical category. It is a pure thought with no necessary reference to sense. It is a pure universal which characterizes any object at any level of spirit so far as that object has a certain degree of intelligibility; but it also characterizes the Absolute. The Absolute may turn out to be far more than a single identity in diversity, but as that at least it must define itself.

Roughly and provisionally it might be said that a form of Nature or Concrete Spirit is a category partially distorted by its embodiment in matter; or it is so much of a category as is manifested to philosophical thought directed upon the spheres of Nature and the human spirit.

6·3. But here the reader's comment is easily anticipated. He will ask why it is not equally true to say that the form of Nature or Concrete Spirit is the pure category enriched by phenomenal embodiment. For if logic is not the whole of philosophy but has in the philosophies of Nature and Concrete Spirit its essential complement, then surely in them there must be some integral element besides a blurred or distorted repetition of the categories, besides a mere attenuated simulacrum which could add nothing to the original. Or is the truth that the antithesis of abstract and concrete, the age-long controversy in which those terms have sometimes actually exchanged their meanings, remains after all unresolved by Hegel? Was it in vain that he restored from sense to thought the moment of intuition? Are we confronted with no more than a new shape of the old Aristotelian dilemma? Have we but another hierarchy whose culminating stage, the postulated norm of all the ascending scale, must either lose something of its perfection to pay the price of immanence, or else break in utter severance away, to become in the end an empty thing-in-itself which we think but cannot know?

Perhaps, though Hegel had no fear of it. But before even the outline of his answer can become clear, something must be said of how the categories relate to one another within the Logic: some account must be given of Hegel's dialectical method.

X

DIALECTIC

1. WE have seen that Hegel restores to thought the intuitive factor in knowledge, the moment of immediate existence and individuality, which Kant had confined, at least in respect of human knowing, to passive sensibility.

In thus denying the Kantian divorce between thinking and knowing, in thus giving a far more real meaning to that activity which Kant had continued to attribute to thought emasculated of its intuitional moment, Hegel in a sense returns to a position common to all Kant's greatest predecessors. In different forms the conception of intuitive thought is present equally in Aristotle and in Descartes, Spinoza, and Leibniz. But none of those thinkers had, in Hegel's view, clearly grasped either (a) the general nature of intuition, or (b) its relation to discursion within the nature of thought itself. We may perhaps roughly summarize their views as follows.

1.1. (a) Aristotle's νοῦς, rational intuition, is an activity one with what it knows, and here is possibly the least one-sided characterization of intellectual intuition to be found before Hegel. But it is still naïve. To Descartes it comes natural to describe intuition as clear and distinct apprehension, because he still conceives that philosophy must agree with, if not subordinate itself to, the theological concept of revelation: the Cartesian intuition is passive. The same is, I think, in the end true of Leibniz. Spinoza's non-Christian conception of *scientia intuitiva* is peculiar and difficult, but to Hegel, at any rate, Spinoza seemed near to the reduction of all things to God's eternal knowing. Kant's (of course quite problematic) intuitive intelligence was one creative of its own object. 'Creative' does not mean to Kant 'practical', but Kant's thought is probably coloured by the theological conception of creation.

As against these modern thinkers Hegel saw in the religious view of the world a form of experience less complete than philosophy. His conception of thought as intuitive is an effort to expand the Aristotelian νοῦς, and to surpass both

the view of thought as illuminant[1] and the idea of it as
creative.

(*b*) At least in Aristotle and Descartes intuition tends to
become wholly severed from discursion. We seem to be
presented with a number of self-evident truths whose connexion with the consequences supposed to follow from them
thus becomes inexplicable. We are confronted with a
dilemma: either inference is a tautologous *petitio principii*, or
it is an inconsequent leap to a fresh intuition.[2]

1·2. Hegel's conception of thought as dialectical is an
attempt to solve this dilemma. His hope is to show that it
arises from conceiving two moments of a unity in abstract
separation. Thought is intuitive, but so far *merely* immediate.
It is discursive, but this *discursus* is its own activity of self-
mediation. Moreover, this mediation is a self-development
towards new immediacy which mediation enriches; a progress and yet a return upon itself. This whole activity,
verbally expressed as if it were three temporally successive
phases, is real only in the union of the first and second
moment in the third.

Hegel, in short, regards thought as dialectical because it
is the supreme and truest form of that activity which is the
essential nature of spirit self-constituent in human experience. But we can best understand the immense reconstruction of familiar ways of thinking which the dialectical method
involves if we follow tradition, and to a large extent Hegel
himself, by treating it in a more or less familiar terminology.
The principle of Hegel's dialectic in its formal and *prima
facie* most prominent shape is the synthesis of opposites.[3]

2. If there were anything utterly new in this principle
it could not belong to Hegel's philosophy. Practically all
the early Greek thinkers—'as if', says Aristotle, 'compelled
by truth itself'—had recognized the importance of opposites in the constitution of the universe. Aristotle himself
had taken matter-*qua*-privation and form as the primary

[1] Which, incidentally, can be found both in Plato and Aristotle.
[2] See ch. iv, § 4·4 above. The *Regulae* of Descartes offers a theory of demonstration which entails much the same difficulties as Aristotle's.
[3] Opposition is a category of Essence. Hence, the reader will note that this
phrase has only a very general sense.

contrariety of his natural world,[1] and he had constructed the four elements out of contrary qualities. He had conceived the properties of species as capacities in the specimen of change between contrary poles, and he often observes that the knowledge of contraries is one and the same. His assertion of the synthesis of opposites as the identity of subject and object in fully actual knowing, in the perfect activity of God's self-consciousness, constitutes in Hegel's eyes the summit of his speculation. Plato had only succeeded in stating it in terms of his relatively abstract Forms. Real as the Platonic Forms are, they are not, as Aristotle complained, efficient or final causes of the particulars which partake in them. They and the Pythagorean numbers, to which they are closely akin, are something less, in Hegel's view, than the fuller Aristotelian conception of reality as activity.

2·1. It is perhaps well to remark in passing that Plato did not, as some critics have supposed, first conceive the Forms as subjective abstract concepts and then proceed to 'reify' or hypostatize them; nor does Hegel by calling the Forms 'abstract' mean to imply that he did. It is essential to the comprehension equally of Plato, Aristotle, and Hegel himself to grasp that, although all three of them regard the universal as essentially the intelligible, yet no one of them is in the position of starting with a nominalist view of the universal as peculiarly 'mental', and then struggling to put it back somehow into 'reality'. To Hegel Plato's Forms are relatively abstract because they fail to exhibit the universal as activity, not because they are 'mental' concepts. On the other hand, the consequence of this failure of course is that, although the Forms are vehemently asserted by Plato to be 'really real', and are certainly not abstract in the sense of being either mental concepts or common characters divorced from difference, yet they remain less than the full nature of reality, and the door is opened to two different possible interpretations of them: Either (*a*) the Forms, as Aristotle complained, subsist in a real world of their own as absolute singulars which are real but not real enough to have efficacy in the world we experience; or (*b*) they become purely subjective 'mental' concepts, quite external to the real object

[1] Cf. ch. ii, § 6 above.

of thought. Plato, in point of fact, explicitly denies that the
Form is a subjective concept (νόημα), and the first interpretation is much the nearer to his actual way of thinking. Nevertheless, the second interpretation is really only the obverse
of the first: a 'mere thought' and an 'imperfect reality' are
simply the two sides of a phase of Concrete Spirit in which
subject and object do not yet fully coincide.

2·2. To return from this digression. Although Hegel
sees in Aristotle's conception of reality as activity an advance
on Plato's Forms, yet the detail, if not the spirit, of his dialectic owes less to Aristotle than to Plato. To Aristotle substance has no contrary, and God, for all that the knowledge
of contraries is one, no knowledge of evil. Although his
Scala Universi is a developing series in which opposites play
an important part, the synthesis of opposites is not the principle of its development. In other words, Aristotle, though
he asserts perfect thought to be the synthesis of opposites,
does not fully succeed in expressing his *Scala* in the medium
of thought.[1] Plato, on the other hand, did in his later
dialogues begin to experiment with the Forms as syntheses
of opposites. One positive result of his extremely obscure
Parmenides appears to be that certain pairs of Forms, such
as One and Many, Whole and Parts, &c., are not predicable
in mutual exclusion of one another, as empirical predicates
are. Among these pairs of Forms which are not mutually
exclusive are Being and Not-being, and it is Plato's conception of this particular pair of opposites which is specially
significant for Hegel's conception of dialectic. But though
Hegel regards the *Parmenides* as Plato's dialectical master-
piece,[2] this union or 'communion', as Plato calls it, of Being
and Not-being is, in fact, far more clearly worked out in the
Sophist.

2·3. In the *Sophist* Plato tries openly to meet the difficulty
raised by the Eleatic dialecticians. The Eleatics, maintaining
with Parmenides that only Being *is* and can be thought, held
that to say 'A is B' is to utter a senseless contradiction,
and that to say 'A is not B' is to predicate not-being, and

---

[1] Cf. HΦ, JE, xviii, p. 333: 'Aristotle speaks of νοῦς, but not of any special
nature of νοῦς.'

[2] Yet is aware of its defects; cf. LL, i, p. 53.

therefore to predicate nothing at all; i.e. both affirmative and negative judgement are impossible. Plato does not, as some logicians have done, attempt to solve the deadlock by suggesting that the 'is' of predication and the 'is' of existential judgement are homonyms—surely the most stultifying fallacy ever propounded in logic. He replies that the negative judgement in point of fact predicates not nothing at all but 'otherness', and that that predication is genuinely significant judgement. 'A is not B' means that A is significantly other than B. i.e. B is a real character excluded from A, and not-B is not nonentity but a real character which A possesses through excluding B. Further, since there is no predicate which cannot be significantly excluded so that its negation characterizes some subject, it follows that not-being, in the sense of significant otherness, must characterize all that (also) is. It must, says Plato, have as many parts as knowledge. Whatever *is* also *is not*, in the sense of being other than something else and of significantly characterizing that something else by being other than it. Hegel remarks that this otherness, this capacity of any and every thing to enter judgement as a negative predicate, is well expressed in the Latin idiom *aliud aliud*.

2·4. Plato's further treatment in the *Sophist* of these opposites is not perfectly clear.[1] Plato inherited from Socrates the general conception of thought as a dialectic of question and answer, the 'conversation of the soul with herself' which moves by developing its initial premiss through contradiction into a concrete whole, a καθόλου. In his myth of ἀνάμνησις he had expressed the dialectical conception that the goal of thinking is somehow present in germ at the start; that we always come to know not something simply new but something which we knew less well before. But his effort, first formulated in the *Republic*, to transform it into a full-grown philosophical method remained incomplete. So far as can be judged from the dialogues, Plato on the whole conceived the dialectical activity of thinking as centred in a soul which remains merely akin to, and not ultimately one with, the Forms; and the Forms in consequence remain relatively inactive and abstract. If this was Plato's position,

[1] See my *Aristotle*, pp. 52 ff.

it is not surprising that Aristotle, though he conceived fully active knowing as a coincidence of opposites, should have relegated dialectic to a level of thinking below both philosophy and special science; that he should have treated coming to know as throwing no special light on knowing. In *Physics*, vii. 3, he asserts that there is no coming to be of knowledge, only a stabilizing of the individual soul upon which knowledge supervenes.

2·5. Nevertheless, Plato had made the most important discovery in the history of logic. He had seen that to have determinate character is to be determinable by position, but determinate by negation. If I may be forgiven a loose metaphor, Aristotle's conception of activity is the soul of Hegel's system, but the Platonic doctrine of negation is its life blood. Negation is for Hegel the general name for determinateness as such: although anything—any finite thing or the Absolute itself—must *be* in order to be determinate, yet nothing could have any character at all without being significantly other.[1] For Hegel the synthesis of subject and object in self-consciousness is the clue to all experience, and in this all-pervasive opposition and coincidence of Being and Not-being he finds it in its most abstract categorical form. Being and Not-being are the first two categories of Hegel's Logic, the elements which constitute the first and simplest synthesis of opposites.

We have now to see how this is so. Once again we may most easily start from a position near to common sense, although this will involve some digression and repetition.[2]

3. If we believe Hegel, we must hold that thought has its own moment of intuition; that it expresses itself in a far greater number of categories than Kant supposed; that these categories lack neither native content nor their own proper

---

[1] The converse of the Spinozistic dictum, *Determinatio est negatio*. Contrast the view of Kant, who regarded the difference between affirmation and negation as a difference in the form of thought wholly irrespective of its content: 'No doubt all propositions may *logically* be expressed as negative; but when we come to the question whether the contents of our knowledge are enlarged or restricted by a judgment, we find that the proper business of negative judgments is solely to prevent error.' KRV, B, p. 737.

[2] In reading what follows, ch. viii, especially §§ 3·2–3·3 and § 5·7, should be borne in mind.

interconnexion; that, further, the categories interconnect because they are phases in the single activity of spirit immanent in any finite experience, and that if we reflect on any finite experience we shall discover it to be essentially self-transcending, just because this immanent activity constitutes it.

If this is so, the logician's reflection upon the activity of the Understanding in our empirical thinking must in principle ultimately reveal all the categories. Such reflection is, in fact, the only possible method of eliciting that articulate totality which the categories must on Hegel's view present when seen in their *native* interconnexion as phases of spirit's activity. A very careless reading of Hegel's Logic might perhaps leave the impression that, because Hegel regards thought as self-developing, therefore the whole series of categories ought to flow with such strict necessity that any one who clearly grasped the first could deduce all the rest by mechanical application of a rule and without reference to empirical thinking. There could be no more false conception of the necessity with which categories follow one another. They are not, indeed, on Hegel's view, subject to verification in empirical experience, but that is because their real relation to empirical thinking is precisely the reverse of that. The categories are the truth of empirical thought, that which the empirical thinker, could he become fully self-conscious, would find to be the whole and sole nature of his thought. Hence logical reflection upon empirical thinking is, historically speaking, a quite indispensable preliminary to the construction of the Hegelian Logic. The natural history of thought, as Hegel entitles formal logic, the Kantian transcendental logic, and in principle any logic which springs from serious reflection on thinking at any level, are all necessary stages on the way to an explicitly philosophical logic. Hegel does not regard those logicians who retain the standpoint of the Understanding as making no contribution to the subject. On the contrary, his own Logic is always the reconstruction of their work, never its mere abolition. His frequent polemic against them is excited in the main by the abstract and limited view of thought's nature which they offer as final because they have scarcely risen above that level of thinking which they wish to interpret. Even Kant failed to elevate his philosophical thinking wholly above the empirical level, although he made a vitally important advance when he taught that the empirical synthesis, the field of more or less casually associated objects which centres round an experient's focus of attention, presupposes the transcendental synthesis of thought and imagination.

3·1. The empirical thinker is satisfied if he reaches a conclusion upon which he can act, or one which satisfies an always limited theoretical curiosity. The truth which contents him answers only the question which he has put, and answers it in the terms in which he has put it. He attempts to verify or disprove an ideal, and therefore universal, suggestion in empirical experience—to test, as he will say, the correspondence of his idea with a real object independent of his thinking. But the selective control which he has exercised on that object escapes his notice, and he does not realize that he gets his answer always in the form of a particular judgement which asserts no more than that there is a case, or that there are some cases, in which his universal suggestion is true or false. Even if he is a man of science, this is still in large measure so, and in any case his pursuit of scientific truth is confined to a sphere sharply abstracted from the richness of everyday thinking. He must ignore the hypothetical nature of all his thought. He must forget that his premisses are borrowed, and the fuller implications of the conclusion he reaches, or of the judgements he makes on the way to it, do not concern him. He must treat them as irrelevant if he is to get the truth he wants. If he were not unconscious that he selects, and so also—inevitably— modifies and reconstitutes both the general field of his inquiry and the object to which he appeals as to an independent witness for the verification or disproof of his idea, he would not be thinking empirically. As an empirical thinker his self-consciousness is confined to that consciousness of himself as bare subject which is given in Kant's transcendental unity of apperception; to the mere awareness of that 'I' which accompanies every act of his thought, but remains, so to say, behind the head as a blank form of universality whereof nothing in detail can be said precisely because it cannot be made an object.

3·2. It is thus almost tautologous to say that the empirical thinker, so long as he is sure of what the precise subject of his inquiry is, and so long as he has the confidence to ask a definite question demanding a precise yes or no, must repudiate the suggestion that his thought is self-transcending. To accept it would be to admit that he never had reached, and never could reach, the truth which he desired.

Yet the very slightest logical reflection, the least effort of the Understanding to comprehend itself, finds puzzles in the procedure of the commonest thinking. The fear, e.g., that all inference may be either a leap in the dark or a *petitio principii* is as old as logic. Such puzzles have their origin in the fact that for the empirical thinker himself his thought can never be self-transcending, and that, nevertheless, it always in a measure does transcend itself even in reaching those limited and abstract conclusions in which alone he is interested. Hence the logician who rises but a little above the empirical level is in a dilemma. If he has got beyond the notion of logic as an art of thinking, he may be well aware that the interest which governs his own thinking as a logician is of a different kind from the interest of the empirical thinker, and he may not shrink from describing thought in terminology which he knows the empirical thinker will not easily recognize. At the same time he is endeavouring to describe thought strictly in terms of the shape it takes in so far only as it yields that limited truth which is all that the empirical thinker desires. Hence, in the self-transcendence which belongs even to the most rudimentary finite thinking he finds not the presence of a more than finite activity but a puzzle which he tasks his wits to solve at the level on which it arises. He does not perceive that finite thinking *qua* merely finite can interest nobody but the finite thinker, and the finite thinker knows better than any logician what his own thinking in its mere finitude is. Thus, unless logic is a teachable art of thinking—a view which has not been found easy to justify—the logician's industry, if it be in fact what he takes it to be, is purely otiose. Whether he be a formal logician or the exponent of an inductive logic of truth, he is, like the empirical thinker, largely ignorant of what it is he does. His real and indispensable contribution to logic con-

sists first in his scientific classification of thought-forms
which prepares the ground for philosophic construction, and
secondly in the discovery of puzzles which he cannot himself
solve.

If, then, there is some self-transcendence in empirical
thought, because in it the activity of spirit is immanent and
constitutive, even a cursory examination of it should reveal
some rough approximation to the general structure and
movement of pure thought which it is the ultimate task of a
philosophical logic to exhibit.

4. In any empirical negative judgement the characterization of the subject by exclusion is never more than partial.
To be other than B never covers the whole nature of A,
where A is the subject of an empirical negative judgement:
a separate field remains for further negative predicates and
also for positive predicates of A which present themselves as
devoid of significant relation to B. Yet in empirical negative
judgement the degree of precision with which the subject is
characterized does vary. To take a familiar example, 'The
soul is not a fire-shovel nor a ship in full sail' is a judgement
in which the subject is scarcely characterized at all, and one
which expresses ignorance as well as knowledge. On the
other hand, in the judgement, 'Circulating blood (excluding
blood in the aorta) which is bright red is not venous', the
subject is precisely qualified as arterial. In this second
judgement it becomes evident that the real content of the
thinking is a system within which dark-venous and bright-
arterial are mutually relevant contrary opposites. The same
fact can be expressed indifferently either by an affirmative
or a negative predicate. This system becomes explicit in the
disjunctive judgement, 'Circulating blood is either venous
and dark or arterial and bright', in which without violation
of the law of contradiction the subject differentiates itself
in two contrary characters.

4·1. But the judgement is still empirical. It is a judgement of the Understanding, which reconstitutes sense-
perception in thought, but must leave a residual sensuous
content unabsorbed, because the distinctive characteristic
of the Understanding is its assumption that its object exists
independent of it and indifferent to it. The form of this

judgement is the truest which judgement of the Understanding can possess. In form its subject and predicate are
fully congruent; for it expresses a subject exhaustively
differentiated in two characterizing predicates which are
mutually determining contraries. Moreover, within this
system of a subject exhaustively particularized in its two
predicates the members of the disjunction are not merely
contraries but also contradictories. Within the system contrariety, contradiction, and precise reciprocal determination
are exactly coincident in meaning.[1] Thus, in respect of
coherence (truth of form) the Understanding can express
itself in no higher type of judgement. On the other hand, in
respect of its content this judgement, being still empirical,
is not fully true. The precision of the disjunction and the
prima facie complete congruence of subject and predicate
depend upon an abstraction. The judgement is defective in
truth of comprehensiveness; for the whole nature of circulating blood is not in point of fact exhausted in the coupled
pair of opposites, 'either dark-venous or bright-arterial'. In
coherence, or form, the judgement is true, but it is not without qualification true as it stands; for its content is only true
given the provisional assumption that two selected characters
of the subject can be treated as quite unaffected by other
characters which the subject is known to possess, and that in
none of its characters is the subject affected by relation to
(in the first instance) other special elements in the organism.

4·11. The reader will observe that coherence as truth of
form is the identity of thought in its *own* difference, the
identity-in-difference of a thought which is not *in se* unintuitive and empty but concretely universal. Hence in
coherence as form there is already the native content of
thought itself. Yet the content of an empirical disjunctive
judgement is not pure thought; it is in large measure
sensuous. This does not, however, mean that the element of
content in it is eked out with sense-matter which comes with
its own differentiations from an alien source. Certainly we

---

[1] Contradictory characters divide the universe between them and simply
exclude one another: 'B and not-B'. But within the system the contrary
characters are also and *eo ipso* contradictories: A and B are contraries, but not-A
is B, and not-B is A.

do in empirical thinking take our world as independent of us, but the defect in truth of content whereof the empirical thinker is conscious is lack of comprehensiveness; and we need not as logicians have raised ourselves very far above the level of empirical thought to see that this lack is a failure to determine the object exhaustively *by thought*, not a want of alien sense-matter. The content of empirical judgement is sensuous and alien for the empirical thinker only so far as his thinking fails to reconstitute it as thought-content.

4·2. Even in empirical thinking the demand of thought to be truth which shall be true both in form and content (be both fully coherent and fully comprehensive) makes itself felt. And it does so, if I may repeat what I have already emphasized, because even in the Understanding there operates as final and formal cause a thinking which is more than Understanding; so that in some measure even Understanding transcends itself and cannot remain wholly unself-conscious in its activity. But Understanding can never satisfy its own demand, and will commonly profess that it asks for no such thing. For its object-world is indifferent to it and, as Kant made abundantly clear, presents itself always as an inexhaustible regress of conditions radiating from the subject's point of sensuous contact with it. Hence when it begins to reflect, it is never sure what really is its criterion of truth. As natural science, it may work under the notion of reducing its object to a single coherent system of classification by division, which shall be at least comprehensive enough to cover the realm of a single special science. Or it may aim at a single system of laws. But it may then, finding itself faced everywhere with indefinite regress, accept the dispersion of its unitary ideal into a plurality of externally related systems, each *merely* other than the rest. Lost in discursion, it takes its intuition to be purely passive and regards its object-world as independently self-subsistent. Thus it falls back for its criterion of truth upon the correspondence of its own thought with this independent object, forgetting that it can never establish this independence, and that if it could, it would have thereby effectually placed one of the supposed corresponding terms out of the range of correspondence. Again, ignorant that its own activity is a reconstituting of sense, it will very often claim that sense-perception yields a clinching correspondence-test of truth in the shape of 'verification'.

4·3. Yet these efforts of the Understanding at self-interpretation are evidence of what the Understanding is, for they do show what the empirical thinker, not attempting reflective interpretation but thinking his proper object, must take truth to be. In common-sense thinking, whether intensified and specialized or not as natural science, there is no guarantee that comprehensiveness and coherence will grow *pari passu*; the one may be only securable at the cost of the other. There is no *a priori* certainty that an empirical truth which finds expression in two disjunct members will have to be taken as truer than one which expresses itself as a disjunctive totality of more than two.[1] Where there is still sensuous content there is a residue of brute fact, and the extent to which sense-perception is to be counted as an independent source of evidence can never be determined on principle. Neither unspecialized common-sense thinking nor special science can dispense with external relations and divorce of quality from relation. Without some use of these abstractive devices they cannot proceed at all. At every point empirical thinking expresses ignorance as well as knowledge. Because sense is not wholly transcended in it but remains in part a function co-operating with thought, the starting-point of empirical thinking is arbitrary. The empirical thinker finds himself at a beginning and cannot tell how he came there; finds himself at an end which does not tell him where he must look to find a fresh beginning.[2] The subject of his judgement is always a limited one, and he cannot say how it came to be thus precisely limited. That is distinctive of empirical thought, and therefore the necessity of its movement is hypothetical and so contingent.

[1] In point of form the disjunctive couple is truer than the disjunctive totality of several members, because in the latter no two members can fully determine each other: each member must preserve against any other given member an aspect or moment of *mere* otherness in order to support its relation of significant otherness to the rest. On the other hand, it would be absurd to try and decide whether the green and red lights of a railway signal embody a truer system than the red, green, and amber lights of a road-traffic signal.

[2] See *Phän.* JE, ii, p. 55.

Nevertheless, the criterion of truth as form, i.e. as coherence, is always operative in empirical thinking, and it is the working of that criterion in the Understanding which shows it to be after all something more than its own reflection can teach it that it is. Hence it is consideration of this element of form which best enables a transition from the thought of the Understanding to the dialectical thought of Reason.

4·4. We have seen how in empirical thought the expression of otherness as purely external relation, or again as a merely vaguely determined difference, betokens nothing but ignorance. The subject of empirical thinking is always limited, and the truest form of judgement which it reveals is a disjunction of two mutually determining members which are at once contrary and contradictory opposites: for each member to be itself is *eo ipso* to be not the other. This progress in truth of form from simple affirmative and simple negative judgement to disjunctive judgement is achieved by widening a limited subject to support two mutually determining predicates. But this coincidence of opposites belongs primarily to the form of the judgement; the content is only harmonious with the form on condition of a provisional abstraction from context.

5. If the exhaustive differentiation of a subject into two mutually determining predicates is the fullest truth of form which empirical judgement reveals, the relation of category to category cannot fall short of this. But whereas in empirical thought systematic disjunction of two members is achieved by widening a limited subject, and at the cost of a provisional abstraction, this procedure can no longer be apposite when the predicates are not empirical characters but categories which all *ex hypothesi* characterize the same single subject, being all definitions of Absolute Spirit.

Hegel's solution is to maintain that the categories differ from one another in degree of concreteness. Each defines the Absolute, but they present an order of development from abstract to concrete.

6. The full meaning of this solution can only emerge gradually, but it may be helpful to anticipate one or two of its implications. It implies that empirical thought expands

its content, as it were, on the flat, because the object of Understanding confronts the subject as a world independently self-subsistent and indifferently real throughout;[1] whereas thought which is possessed of its own full nature—philosophic thought—is in essence self-development from abstract to concrete. It is a process upwards, if we hold to the spatial metaphor, which is contained and realized in its conclusion. Such thought is self-consciousness; a self-positing and self-determining activity, and not the endless hypothetical mapping of an independent object-world in which the fixing of co-ordinates is always arbitrary.[2]

But we must not move too fast. The categories are to be a developing series, and the relation between categories is to be one of opposition at once contrary and contradictory. How Hegel fulfils these conditions we have now to see.

[1] i.e. there are for the Understanding no degrees of reality, no diverse modes of being.

[2] This may be compared with what was said of Aristotle's method in philosophy in ch. iv, § 4·5. Dialectic takes the place of demonstration when the real is conceived as active subject instead of substance. Aristotle only partially achieved the latter transition.

XI

DIALECTICAL LOGIC

1. It follows from the conclusions reached in the last chapter that Hegel's dialectical logic must start with the most abstract possible definition of Absolute Spirit, and that the second category must be the opposite of the first, at once its contrary and contradictory. With these two categories we shall have a content adequate to the ideal form of the disjunctive judgement: an affirmative and a negative judgement having the same subject will unite to differentiate that subject exhaustively in two mutually determining characters.

But with the union of these two characters we shall have, in fact, passed from judgement to inference. Even in empirical experience judgement is always implicit inference. For even there thought is one indivisible movement. A first immediate content is posited only to be mediated, only to be differentiated in a subject and predicate of judgement; the differentiation in which judgement consists passes at once to integration in a system, and that whole movement is inference.

1·1. Thus even in the realm of empirical thinking inference is in principle an integral movement of thought through the mediation of judgement to re-synthesis in system. This follows, indeed, from what was said in the last chapter. But the Understanding is not fully aware of it. Because the Understanding still depends upon sense and does not freely determine its own starting-point, this starting-point tends to become for it a fixed premiss necessitating a conclusion which is not a development of the premiss.[1] In mathematics, where sense seems least to intrude, the starting-point seems specially secure, and the Understanding has there commonly claimed deduction for its method, and rejected altogether the suggestion that its thinking is still empirical. Where sense has still to be acknowledged, and the Understanding proceeds from observation, it has usually proclaimed its method to be inductive; but mistrusting its sensuous partner, whom it cannot feel sure of reducing to the status

[1] Cf. ch. iv, § 4·4 above.

of a perfectly subservient instrument, it has, as a rule, felt far less confidence in the truth of its inductive conclusions. But in both cases it tends to forget the hypothetical, and so contingent, nature of a reasoning which flows from a starting-point not freely determined by itself. Both its deduction and its induction are defective shapes—complementary mutilations—of the true form of inference, which is development as and to system. This is, of course, not to say that Understanding can dispense with using now the one and now the other, any more than it can avoid expressing itself now in a higher, now in a lower form of judgement. For it has to satisfy the claims of truth to be both coherent and comprehensive, claims which must continue to conflict for a thinking which in part absorbs but still in part co-operates with sense, and accords its object-world an indifferent self-subsistence.

2. The disjunctive judgement by its form reveals clearly that judgement is implicit inference—its 'either-or' stops only just short of asserting 'both, but as differents mutually determining one another in a system'. Hence, when philosophic thought finds its fullest expression in the developing series of logical categories, it must fully realize the ideal to which the Understanding in its inference approximates. Consequently neither the positing of an affirmative category without its opposing negative, nor the mere opposition of affirmative and negative categories, will reflect the nature of philosophic thinking. One affirmative category by itself has nothing to offer but the mere simple immediacy which is the focus of sense; affirmative and negative categories in mere opposition would show only the sheer mediation, the differentiation of immediacy, in which judgement, so far as it is not inference, consists. Nothing less than explicit synthesis of opposites differentiated out of immediacy—only, i.e., inference in its fully genuine form as a conclusion containing and realizing its premiss—can express at all the indivisible activity of dialectical Reason which philosophic thinking is.

2.1. Thus the third category will be the explicit synthesis of the opposites in which the first category has issued. The categories, therefore, will not be a discrete series, but will fall

—though not, as we shall see, fall apart—into triadic groups, each consisting of what Hegel, following Fichte, calls thesis, antithesis, and synthesis. To criticize a single category by itself is to attempt to retain in philosophic reasoning the form of sense; even to consider a pair of opposed categories in abstraction from their synthesis is to remain in servitude to the Understanding. Anything said of the first category of a triad without reference to the second and third categories, or again anything said of its thesis and antithesis without mention of their synthesis, signifies merely proleptically or it does not signify at all.

3. It is specially important to remember this in discussing the first triad of Hegel's logic, which, whether it is in the end defensible or not, has provoked a mass of wholly irrelevant comment.

Hegel, as we have already seen, selects for his first pair of opposites Being and Not-being. That the Absolute simply *is*—that is its most abstract possible definition, its minimal characterization. Pure Being is, we may say, the very vanishing-point of characterization; but it is a thought which can be entertained, and therefore it is not below that point. On the other hand, in so far as the Absolute just positively *is* and no more, it has no determinate character—it *is not*. This is not an illusory oscillation between two non-entities, but a real movement of thought. For to think the Absolute as Not-being is, as Plato showed, to think it as 'other'. Whereas in empirical thinking A is A and also significantly other than B, here, so to say, both subject and predicate remain the same, and we are forced to the conclusion that the Absolute *is* and is other than *itself*.[1] In the thought of the Absolute as Not-being pure Being is presupposed; for

[1] It may be well to remind the reader that this is no paradox unless we continue—under the influence of empirical experience—to imagine the Absolute as still a limited thing among other limited things. A finite empirical thing is enabled to be both itself and also significantly other by having another empirical thing in relation to it. This 'supports' its otherness: an empirical thing is determined from without. But beyond the Absolute is nothing by excluding which it can significantly characterize itself. Hence positive Being and Not-being, or otherness, must both characterize the Absolute itself. Nor can we simply deny the analogy from finite things. For if the Absolute is not other than itself, it is and remains utterly featureless and indeterminate.

'otherness', or determinateness in general,[1] presupposes the indeterminate.

3·1. But Being and Not-being are abstractions with only a proleptic meaning. They only become intelligible when they coincide in their synthesis, to which Hegel gives the name of Becoming.

If we conceive the Absolute as that which preserves its self-sameness in and as an endless coming-to-be and perishing of finite things, and next divest that still partly sensuous conception of temporality and of all particular finite content, then what remains as a residue of pure thought will be roughly what Hegel means by Becoming as a self-definition of the Absolute. Absolute Spirit is the concrete identity of subject and object in a timelessly self-consummating activity, and Becoming is the first phase of this activity which is sufficiently concrete to prefigure it as active. Becoming exhibits the first remote analogue of the subject's whole movement of self-alienation and return to itself through its object which was still itself. Yet Becoming is so remote an analogue of activity that it is rather an impotence than an activity, a restless collapse from Being into Not-being and vice versa.

3·11. Hegel's 'Becoming' is not change; for change is temporal, and Time is not a category but a phase of Nature.[2] Becoming is a pure thought, although it is, of course, a category operative in the experience of change.

Becoming, like Being and Not-being, is a part of Hegel's debt to Plato—so far as it is possible to distinguish among Hegel's creditors. But Plato nowhere openly posits dialectical synthesis of Being and Not-being in Becoming, which both to Plato and to Aristotle *is* a form of change. In Hegel's view the dialectic of Plato always remains 'external'; by which he means, I think, that Plato as a dialectician never quite frees himself from the 'detached' attitude of the Understanding.

---

[1] Or better, 'determinability in general'; sheer otherness is no more than that. It is helpful here to recall Aristotle's primary matter and the sheer privation which is its negative moment; cf. ch. ii, § 6·1 above. It should be remembered, too, in this context that matter divorced from form is meaningless: thesis and antithesis are to synthesis as matter is to form.

[2] See ch. viii, § 7 above.

3·2. The triad might be called the *minimum rationale*. But the categories, as was said above,[1] are not a series of discrete triads. The very nature of Reason—which is but another name for Absolute Spirit—is the triple rhythm of its self-negation and re-appropriation of its 'other' self. It is therefore reflected not merely in the three phases of a single triad but also in the relation of triad to triad. The triadic movement of spirit's activity repeats itself with variations on many scales. The first triad is an integral element within the thesis of a larger triad, and so on. Hence, not at any rate until we reach the final synthesis of the Logic can Becoming be wholly intelligible. Only when the self-constitutive and self-conscious activity of spirit has been fully manifested can its first low analogue be clearly grasped.

Meanwhile a further example on a larger scale may help to illustrate the dialectical movement.

4. Quality, Quantity, and Measure (proportion) are the three main phases into which Being, the main thesis of the Logic as a whole, falls. Speaking very roughly, the Absolute defined, or self-defining, as Quality is *simply* a (or the) *quale*. It has, of course, its otherness within it, but positive and negative are here so related[2] that it hardly seems truer to say that, as the dialectic moves, positive simply becomes negative than that negative is simply substituted for positive.[3] Nor is their synthesis truly system; it expresses scarcely more than a reciprocity of transition into one another on the part of thesis and antithesis. The mere *quale* is not a 'thing' distinguishable from a 'quality' which it 'has': it is immediately one with its quality, but only because it is Being in a mode far below the distinction of thing and quality.[4] Its determinateness, what limits its nature, is only that nature itself. It is not determined mediately against and through a genuine other. Imagine the perceptible world lacking any quantitative relations between its sensuous features, so that at the most it exhibits that indefinite regress of 'this' and 'that' and 'that'

---

[1] § 2·1.

[2] 'Relation', like almost every term one is compelled to use in talking of the categories of Being, means too much.

[3] This is more or less true of all the categories of Being.

[4] For the beginning of this conception see my *Aristotle*, p. 72, note 3.

. . . out of which quantitative character will arise but has not yet arisen, and you have roughly the phenomenal embodiment of the category of Quality.

4·1. Quantity is the contradictory of Quality. Measurement is possible only on the assumption that qualitative difference is to be ignored. A quart is a quart, be it of water or of wine. Yet the repetitive character of sense-perception is the presupposition of experiencing number, and man, as Plato saw, takes to counting and measuring in order to understand better the world that he perceives. Of this the logical implication, the underlying thought, is that Quality is the contrary of Quantity, and that in it the germ of Quantity lies hid. Though the Absolute, defined as mere *quale*, contradicts the definition and defines itself as sheer *quantum*, yet the world of Quantity develops out of as well as against the world of Quality.

4·2. The ensuing synthesis of Quality and Quantity Hegel finds in *Mass*, usually translated 'Measure'; i.e. 'measure' in the sense of 'proportion', the Greek ἐμμετρία.

Measure is the thought of the Absolute as a proportioned whole wherein qualitative and quantitative characters are in precise relevance to each other, complete mutual determination; or, better, as a whole in which their opposition is fused without loss or compromise, absorbed not into neutrality but into a higher and richer category. Measure has many phases, but the fusion of qualitative and quantitative difference in a work of art is one phenomenal illustration of this category. The Parthenon is an instance of this interpenetration so astonishing that it must be seen to be believed.[1]

5. Thus the dialectical movement, expressed in terms of a subject-predicate logic, runs as follows. Predicate the minimal positive character of the Absolute, and the precisely opposite (contrary and contradictory) character is seen at once to be a no less true definition of it. But with this insight comes the realization that the Absolute is characterized yet more concretely by the synthesis of these positive and negative predicates. This synthesis is again positive, but with a

---

[1] Aristotle's definition of virtue of character as a mean, often unintelligently criticized as purely quantitative, affords an illustration of Measure in another sphere.

positivity enriched by negation, inasmuch as it contains the original positive character within itself.

Hegel sometimes expresses this by calling the movement of thought to synthesis 'negation of negation'; i.e. not a mere cancellation restoring the original affirmation, but a development to a fresh and genuinely determinate positive.

5·01. To express the movement from thesis through antithesis to synthesis Hegel uses the word *aufheben*. Among its ordinary meanings are (1) to cancel or annul, and (2) to preserve. Hegel uses it to mean both together. The thesis is cancelled as such by the antithesis, but preserved with the antithesis in the synthesis. The synthesis is thus, in Aristotelian terminology, the developed and actualized form of thesis and antithesis. They are its proximate matter. As Hegel puts it, they are 'ideal moments' *aufgehoben*, cancelled-and-preserved, in the synthesis. In one passage[1] Hegel, in describing the transition of one *Volksgeist* into another, expands the second moment of *aufheben* by calling it 'erhalten und verklären', to preserve and to transfigure-and-illuminate. Stirling's 'sublation' is a convenient translation of *Aufhebung*.

The phrase 'ideal moment' requires a word of explanation. Hegel often uses the term *reell* to mean relatively self-subsistent being, and contrasts it in this sense with *ideell*. In this contrast *reell* applies to a stage of the dialectic so long as that stage presents itself as self-subsistent, as, so to say, the last word. But as 'sublated' in a higher stage, the stage which was *reell* has now itself only an *ideell* being. It has lost its relative 'reality', and *is* only as an element subordinated within a more concretely developed phase. An *ideell* phase is what Hegel usually means by a 'moment'.

5·2. To return from this digression. The synthesis, though positive, is not yet fully concrete. The contradiction of the opposites is after all not fully reconciled, and the synthesis becomes in its turn a thesis begetting its own antithesis. The Absolute manifests itself as once again characterized equally by an opposite predicate, and again the contradiction must be sublated, reconciled in a synthesis

[1] *ΦH*, Lasson's ed., 1917, vol. i, p. 48.

transcending thesis and antithesis and absorbing the partial truth which each of them held. Hence, the dialectic[1] must develop triadically until a fully concrete synthesis is reached in which the opposition of positive and negative is completely reconciled; i.e. until a definition is reached which is no longer inadequate, and which does not beget its own opposite. Such a definition may be called positive, but it will have not the more or less abstract positivity which its own negation at once opposes, but a fully concrete positivity overcoming and making negation its very own. It will, in fact, be the Absolute self-defining as the activity of thought which has its own concrete thinking for the content of its thought. Hegel calls it the Absolute Idea.

5·3. The detail of Hegel's categories is far too complicated matter for an *Introduction*. The triadic theme, as has already been remarked,[2] repeats itself on many scales, and never without variation. In fact, (*a*) there is development within each triad; (*b*) there is a continuous development from triad to triad; (*c*) the whole series of categories is a triad of three main sections related as thesis, antithesis, and synthesis; (*d*) each of these will again subdivide triadically on a scale smaller than that of the main triad but greater than that of the smallest-scale triads—indeed, on several intervening scales. The general nature of the variation is this. As the dialectic proceeds from more to less abstract definitions of the Absolute, the definitions will at first (in the categories of Being) seem to veer round helplessly into their opposites, cancelled rather than preserved, despite an extreme acuteness of contradiction. Next (in the categories of Essence) we shall find the relation of thesis to antithesis that of identity to diversity, or of immediacy to mediation, rather than that of sheer affirmation to sheer negation. Here the synthesis will show identity in diversity, but in every triad the aspects of cancellation and preservation will be present together and almost in equipoise. Thesis will meet antithesis with a fixity of opposition which seems to resist the transitional move-

---

[1] Hegel sometimes uses the term 'dialectic' in a stricter sense to denote the negative movement of thought from thesis to antithesis, applying to the fully concrete thought of the synthesis the term 'speculative'.

[2] § 3·2 above.

ment of the dialectic.[1] In Being the emphasis was on thesis; in Essence it is on antithesis. When we reach the categories of the Notion, the movement will at every step be explicit development, preservation rather than cancellation: the emphasis will be on synthesis.

5·31. The precise meaning of Notion (*Begriff*) can only become clear as its phases develop in the Logic, but the reader may be puzzled by finding the term used proleptically in the earlier part of the Logic.[2] I have called the triad the *minimum rationale*, and the categories of the Notion are the categories of Reason; i.e. they express explicitly that activity of self-synthesis through self-opposition which Reason is. Hence, any triad of the Logic may be called Notion in a general proleptic sense, and more particularly the synthesis of any triad may be called the notion of its thesis and antithesis. So, too, Hegel will speak of distinctions and processes in Nature, History, Art, &c., as 'notional', so far as they are experienced as rational triads; or, as he usually puts it, so far as self-conscious Reason finds itself in them. And in these spheres he often uses the term 'Universal' as a synonym for Notion. 'The Universal' is the first triad of notional categories, and the usage marks Hegel's conception of the universal as essentially concrete.

It follows that the unavoidable use of singular and plural number in reference to the terms Notion and Universal demands a flexible interpretation, and this is *a fortiori* true of the term 'category' or *Denkbestimmung*, which in one context of the Logic will signify any single small-scale thesis, antithesis, or synthesis, in another a whole 'section' of small-scale triads.

---

[1] The categories of Being are the lower categories of the Understanding; they are the thought which sense-perception embodies. The categories of Essence are the higher categories of the Understanding; they are thought distinct from sense, but still explicitly based upon it. This contrast reflects the distinction which Kant maintains between (*a*) the categories of quality and quantity, and (*b*) the categories of relation and modality. Kant puts it forward again in respect of the schematized categories as the difference between (*a*) mathematical and constitutive principles, and (*b*) dynamical and regulative principles. Yet Hegel's modification of this Kantian distinction is very great; in particular, all Hegel's categories of Being and Essence reconstitute sense as thought, they do not inform an alien sense-matter.

[2] See, however, meanwhile ch. xiv, §§ 1–3·2.

5·4. It may be asked how far Hegel succeeds in justifying this claim of each category and each transition to be interpreted through and through in the light of the whole because each is one pulse in a single activity. But that question cannot be answered while we have before us no more than a rough account of one or two triads. To object to Hegel's Logic either that it is not an organic whole, or that it is too much of one, is not pertinent until the whole has been deeply studied. At any rate, its movement is individualized with astonishing breadth and subtlety at every step.

5·5. Hegel conceives not merely the categories but also the forms of Nature and Concrete Spirit as phases of a dialectical movement. At the beginning of Chapter IX it was observed that the relation of the Logic to the Philosophies of Nature and Spirit was a crux of Hegelian exegesis, and in Chapter IX, § 6·3, I confessed the difficulty of seeing precisely how a form of Nature or Concrete Spirit compares with a logical category. Now that we have seen something of the dialectical method the problem arises at a further stage, and the reader will demand to know how the dialectic of these forms compares with and relates to the dialectic of the categories.

But again I must beg leave to postpone a direct answer. One great lesson of the dialectical method is that no question can be answered until it is put in its proper form. If there is any satisfactory answer to the reader's demand, the question itself must first be shaped through the more detailed investigation of Hegel's Logic which I propose to attempt in a further work on Hegel.

Meanwhile there is still ground to be cleared by the discussion of certain points of contrast between Hegel's conception of logic and logical doctrines of less ambitious and *prima facie* safer scope.

XII
DIALECTICAL AND OTHER LOGICS

1. IT has been objected to Hegel's Logic that he bases it on a flat denial of the law of contradiction.

The objection suggests that this law is for logic an unexaminable universal axiom to be accepted as an *a priori* datum. But if it is, there is exempted from the logician's critical scrutiny what is implied by this very objection to be an extremely important character of thought. Hegel has plenty to say of the law of contradiction in its place *within* logic,[1] nor does he there deny its truth. The law of contradiction is a *Denkbestimmung*. Like any other *Denkbestimmung*, it is a phase in the activity which thought is. It is not a law inexplicably imposed upon thought; nor is it a character of thought fundamental or axiomatic, if that is to mean that other characters of thought throw no light on it when the logician comes to reflect on them and it together.

1·01. The *prima facie* puzzle which arises over the question how there can be a thinking study of laws or forms of thought is admirably dealt with in the *Zusatz* to EL, § 41 :

'Kant undertook to examine how far the forms of thought were capable of leading to the knowledge of truth. In particular he demanded a criticism of the faculty of cognition (*Erkenntnisvermögen*) as preliminary to its exercise. That is a fair demand if it means that even the forms of thought must be made an object of investigation. Unfortunately there soon creeps in the misconception of already knowing before you know—the error of refusing to enter the water until you have learnt to swim. It is, indeed, true that the forms of thought should be subjected to a scrutiny before they are used: yet what is this scrutiny but *ipso facto* a cognition? So that what we want is to combine in our process of inquiry the activity (*Tätigkeit*) of the forms of thought with a criticism of them. The forms of thought must be studied in their essential nature and complete development: they are at once the object of research and the activity of that object. Hence, they examine themselves: in their own activity they must determine their limits, and point out their defects. This is that activity of thought which will hereafter be specially considered under the name of dialectic; and regarding it we need only at the outset observe that, instead of

---

[1] Among the categories of Essence.

being brought to bear on the categories from without, it is immanent in their own activity.'

The reader should compare Hegel's criticism of the conception of knowledge as an instrument in the opening pages of the Introduction to the *Phänomenologie* (a parallel passage also directed against Kant). The same work contains an illuminating criticism of (*a*) the laws of thought as conceived in common logic, and (*b*) psychological laws of the mind's behaviour, as one-sided abstractions from the full nature of thought.[1]

1·2. The law of contradiction has been variously expounded. As it appears in logics which assume thought to be *par excellence* the thinking of the Understanding, it seems in effect to be this principle: 'A is B' and 'A is not B' cannot both be true if it is assumed that A, as subject of either suggested predication, is absolutely self-identical without difference. The law, thus taken by itself, is the tautologous statement that two different predicates cannot occupy the same predicative position.[2] Where it is true that A is both B and also not B, A is identical *in* difference, and even empirical thinking moves only on the assumption that identity in difference is a fact, even if not a universal fact. If it is assumed to be never a fact, the law is violated by any attribution of two predicates to one subject, *a fortiori* by any disjunctive judgement.

1·3. To any logician who identifies thought with the Understanding the relation of thesis and antithesis in Hegel's Logic is bound to seem a violation of the law of contradiction. For thesis and antithesis are not merely contraries precisely articulating difference; they are also contradictories dividing the universe between them, and so apparently competing for the same predicative position. But though they both claim to characterize the Absolute as a whole, they are not, in fact, competing for the same position; for the subject which they characterize *develops* in the transition from thesis to antithesis. Despite Hegel's occasionally misleading language, the antithesis is not just the negation of the thesis: it is the

---

[1] *Phän.* JE, ii, pp. 233–9.
[2] Taken together dialectically with other *Denkbestimmungen* of the Understanding it is not tautologous.

negated thesis. Even in the case of Not-being this is so, although it only becomes explicit in the synthesis. But if it were not so, no synthesis could supervene; the movement would be dislocated.[1]

Thus, in empirical thinking violation of the law of contradiction is avoided by the expansion in space or time of the logical subject, as it were, on the same level, so that the subject can accept both the offered predicates as compatible; whereas in the dialectical triad there is no violation of the law because the opposites are not on the same level.

1.31. Yet it must be remembered that this distinction between empirical and philosophical thinking is not absolute. If there were in empirical thought no development, no lift from level to level, every empirical proposition would be either false or tautologous. The law of contradiction would have paralysed thought altogether, and when the logical subject strove to expand in order to accept otherwise incompatible predicates, it would simply split into two unrelated subjects. For it is only because it is an identity in difference that the expanding subject remains one: identity in difference always betokens development, and vice versa. Because the Understanding prefigures Reason, yet also still refigures sense, empirical thought is a constant compromise. The field of empirical thinking is always a limited abstraction. Hence, within it there are constant gaps, a constant admission of sheerly external relations there in order to secure connexion here. In the case of inference this is even more obvious. If identity in difference and development be totally denied, all inference is either invalid or *petitio principii*. Even the so-called 'implication' of the logisticians is an unacknowledged ghost of identity in difference.

Moreover, although I have said that the dialectical triad does not violate the law of contradiction, yet it must be observed that the opposites of dialectic reconcile contradiction and contrariety only within their triad. The synthesis of any triad, in fact, becomes thesis to a fresh antithesis only because it has failed fully to reconcile contradiction.

2. It is by now evident that the notion of subject and

---

[1] Cf. ch. xi, § 3·2 above. It cannot be too often emphasized that to Hegel thought is the *unbroken* self-constituting activity of Absolute Spirit.

predicate, which has so far been accepted more or less uncritically in our discussion of Hegel's categories,[1] requires
modification in many respects. In this and the two next
sections we will concern ourselves with two points in connexion primarily with the predicate.

In the eyes of any logician who consistently adopts the
attitude of the Understanding existence is not a predicate,
and the 'is' of existence and the copula, the 'is' of predication,
are homonymous. The subject of the predicative judgement
is (exists), and all its possible predicates presuppose that it *is*.
They determine *what* it is, not *that* nor *how* it is:[2] its being
(existence) is for this type of logician the modeless being
which it shares with any other possible subject of predication,
not anything which varies with its particular nature. Correspondingly the existential judgement is of a totally different
type from the predicative. It simply asserts or denies that
in the universe exists something of which the characters
expressed by its grammatical subject can be predicated truly
in a predicative judgement.[3] This general attitude is common
to the traditional logic of empiricism, to the logisticians,[4] and
also to Kant, since Kant attributes to sense and not to
thought the intuition of reality.

If thought be not devoid of intuition, this doctrine cannot
hold. But the controversy has raged largely in the sphere of
empirical thinking, and has begotten some confusion. From
the standpoint of Hegel, and of any idealist logic which
derives its inspiration from Hegel, Kant and those who in
this respect have followed him are perfectly right in asserting

[1] See ch. ix, § 3·2 above.
[2] i.e. not how it *is*. They may, of course, be relational predicates.
[3] On a Kantian view it will assert or deny that an object is given in intuition
corresponding to what in itself is a mere concept.
[4] I intend 'predicative judgement' to cover all judgement which in any
way determines a subject, and to exclude only existential judgement. The
doctrines of the proposition put forward by logisticians and logical positivists
introduce difficulties of their own (see ch. xiii, § 2·2 below), but a division
of propositions into, e.g., subject and predicate propositions, relational propositions, and class-membership propositions does not, I think, affect the
argument. Propositions with no grammatical subject would also be covered;
see following footnote. For the rather naïve efforts of logistic to solve the
problem of existential judgement, see Professor Stebbing's *Modern Introduction
to Logic*, pp. 157 ff.

that existence is not a predicate. For to assert that existence is a predicate is to assert, absurdly, that it is one among the characters predicable in judgement of a logical subject; to treat it as on all fours with, e.g., liquid predicated of water, or omnipotent predicated of God, and so to consider it as adding something to *what* water or God is. But that is not the end of the matter. In judgement we do not simply assert *what* something is, the existence of which is presupposed as given to intuition in independence of a purely discursive thought: we also in *all* judgement claim truth for the assertion *that* something is. And the intuitive and discursive moments in judgement are quite clearly factors in one activity of *thought*. In judging predicatively we are thinking out *what* x is, and therein further determining the mode in which we may assert *that* x is. Conversely, in existential judgement we are never concerned with the mere being of *x* in the universe—this any subject of judgement must have in order to be thought at all; we always in existential judgement assert or deny that *x*, having a certain determinate *what*, has a certain mode of being.[1] That its object be at once universal and individual is the native demand of thought itself, and the inadequate fulfilment of this demand is the only spring of our thinking. Doubtless it is mere confusion to include the *that*, the being of *x*, within its *what*. To do so is first to distinguish the *what* from the *that*, and then to lump one of two terms, which are only defined by this distinction, into the other. The medieval conception of a being whose essence and existence are one was not the conception of a perfect essence which contained existence as one of its moments. But to deny that in judging predicatively we think that the subject *is* is a worse error than to assert that existence is a predicate.

In short, all judgement is both predicative and existential. The less developed the level of the thinking on which we reflect, the more marked is the discrepancy between these two aspects. To use this discrepancy as a basis for classifying

[1] Hence, the logical subject of any judgement is not necessarily reflected by the grammatical subject of the proposition, but is rather the reality of which we judge the whole content expressed by the nexus of grammatical subject and predicate.

types of judgement, or of proposition, may be legitimate in a natural history of thought, but to forget that the whole nisus of thought is towards its conquest is to court disaster. To call the copulative and the existential 'is' sheer homonyms is to embrace it.

An Hegelian category, since it is a self-definition of spirit, is *eo ipso* a mode of being, a degree of reality as well as—or rather in one with—a character of the real. It at once expresses that and how and what Absolute Spirit is. For Absolute Spirit *is* its categories; they are its self-determinations, not mere characters which it *has*. The view that reality has no degrees, and that reality (or 'existence' or 'being'— the terms are simply synonymous on this view, if indeed they in the end mean anything at all) is given to thought from a source outside thought, belongs only to empirical thinking. Its introduction into philosophical theory is ruinous.

3. It is equally obvious, in connexion with the predicate, that the sharp distinction between qualities and relations maintained by modern formal logic belongs only to empirical thinking. In the pluralistic universe of the Understanding some relations must be held wholly external in order to secure the cohesion of limited systems; 'otherness' cannot be taken everywhere to characterize significantly. But where the 'subject' of all 'predicates' is the same, it is not so. If we have to answer the question whether the Hegelian categories are qualities or relations, we must say that in Hegel's Logic quality and relation are coextensive and coincident; that every category is at once an all-pervasive quality and an all-pervasive relation. But the question is *mal posée*, and the answer therefore loose and unsatisfactory. For quality and relation both fall within the dialectical whole of the Logic: they are integral phases of it, and just because they are they receive within it their proper criticism.

3·1. Thus quality and relation are in the same case as the law of contradiction. To the logician who reflects on empirical thought while himself remaining at the level of the Understanding, quality and relation, like the 'laws of thought', the forms of judgement (or proposition) and inference, and/or whatever other forms seem to him insusceptible of further analysis, do not, when he has once brought them to the light in their simple nakedness, admit of any further criticism. Assuming that he has successfully made explicit these forms or principles which empirical thinking unconsciously accepts, his task of pure analysis is done. These principles are then as unexaminable to him as is his starting-point to the empirical thinker. For though he has so far interpreted empirical thinking as to make explicit some of its implications, he is only a natural historian of thought. He produces results of interest, but he remains with the empirical thinker at the level of the Understanding. If questioned on the subject of metaphysics, he probably begins by maintaining that his logical results are simply indifferent to metaphysical truth, and ends by denying the possibility of metaphysics on the ground that the principles of empirical thought do not warrant it. Nor, indeed, do they: when he asks rhetorically whether any of the principles of traditional metaphysics are capable of empirical verification, he can answer his own question with a confident and perfectly truthful negative. But when he goes on to conclude that they are nonsensical, he fails to see that his own denial of metaphysics has been a metaphysical statement, nor does he inquire whether the principles of empirical thinking themselves require a warrant. Because he remains at the level of the Understanding, he must hold that any such inquiry, any criticism applied to those principles, would itself be a thinking in which they were already assumed and operative, and that such criticism must therefore be totally abortive. He does not realize that he is only asserting the impossibility of interpreting any level of experience without transcending, or 'sublating', it.

4. We may now return to consider the logical subject. Commonly we distinguish between two meanings of the term 'subject', and with the experient subject ordinary logic is not concerned. But the Absolute is not only a subject of predicates; it is a subject self-expressive in the categories, which are phases of its self-consciousness. A logical subject to which an experient subject attributes a predicate as to a thing external to itself is a conception belonging to empirical thought; for there the subject as a bearer of predicates is an object confronting the experient subject. But if the

experient subject is self-definitory, and conscious of itself in and, as its object, then the two senses of 'subject' must coincide. It must, however, be added that, as was the case with quality and relation, the two senses of 'subject' only receive their proper criticism within the Logic.

4·1. A corollary is worth observing. The absolute distinction of kind between knowledge and opinion which realists of the Cook-Wilsonian type maintain, does not hold for Hegel. To him full knowledge is also full certainty, because it is the fulfilling of that certainty which, on a true interpretation, Descartes's *cogito ergo sum* guarantees. The beginning of knowledge is the certainty of Reason that it is all reality.

5. The conclusions of this chapter may be summed thus. The logic of empirical thinking severs sharply from one another (1) universal axioms of thought exempt from criticism; (2) predicates expressing the 'what' but not the 'that' of (3) logical subjects of predication; (4) singular judging subjects. Hegel's Logic sublates these abstract distinctions. The Hegelian category is a phase of active thought. It is an axiom because thought is free and autonomous; it is logical subject and predicate because thought is self-characterizing; it is thinking subject because thought is self-conscious.

XIII

TRUTH: OTHER LOGICIANS AND HEGEL

1. In order to sum up and develop further this transcendence, or sublation, of distinctions which remain rigid and irresoluble in ordinary logic, we may profitably devote this chapter and the next to contrasting Hegel's conception of truth with that of any logician who retains wholly or in part the attitude of the Understanding.

2. The realist theory of knowledge which any logic strictly and solely a logic of the Understanding[1] implies, may perhaps be sketched roughly as follows. To the Understanding, when it attempts to reflect, the mind-independence of its possible objects seems to be the sole and indispensable guarantee of stability and freedom from caprice in thinking. Truth is most commonly taken to be correctness: a thought, or the proposition expressing it, is true in so far as it corresponds correctly to an independent 'thing'; or to an independent 'fact', to the 'thing', i.e., as it is for, but in no way determined by, the experient mind. An exact record by a good scientific instrument is the typical reflection of this 'truth'. A partially true thought (or proposition, or complex of propositions) will correspond with absolute correctness to one or some of the independently real 'things', and fail entirely to correspond to others. For truth *qua* correctness and 'things' *qua* independently real are alike devoid of degree.

2·1. The main presuppositions of any correspondence theory seem to be (1) a plurality of singular minds whose experiencing is essentially adjectival to a mind *qua* singular individual, and (2) a plurality of 'things' or groups of 'things', some totally independent of others, and all of them independent of minds. The position cannot be stated without alternatives, for correspondence theories vary considerably, at any rate on the surface. The correspondence may be taken to relate a 'thing' to a mind directly by a 'not further analysable relation', or (a now rather discredited fashion)

---

[1] This phrase is not here intended to cover Kant's logic. What follows has been to some extent anticipated in ch. x.

through a representative image, or through some other sort
of symbolic go-between. Where a go-between is employed,
opinion as to its precise status—is it 'subjective' or 'objective', 'mental' or 'non-mental'? and so forth—and opinion as
to what is the proper subject of the predicates 'true' and
'false'—is it, e.g., a state of mind or a proposition?—will vary
accordingly.[1]

2·2. Again, there may be some compounding or blurring
of these alternatives, and if the terms 'true' and 'false' be held
applicable only to propositions, then the proposition itself
may perhaps throw up the part of Pandarus and declare its
independence. If that occurs, truth ceases to be a plain
matter of correspondence with external things. Propositions
may, as for a short time Mr. Bertrand Russell held, be said
to 'subsist', possessing in themselves the characters of truth
and falsity. Or, again, with the assistance of a phenomenalism borrowed from Hume rather than from Kant,[2]
propositions may be classified as (i) propositions subject to
probabilification, if not verification, in empirical experience,
(ii) analytic logical propositions which are tautologous but
necessarily implied in all thinking, and (iii) nonsensical
propositions which consist largely of those which embody
the views of one's opponents. Sentences stating 'value
judgements' will express only the emotive state of the
speaker; they will not signify truly or falsely any 'fact'
beyond that. In logical positivism truth is, I suppose, a
character of analytic propositions revealed by rational insight
which carries with it unquestionable certainty, and a character
which some empirical propositions may justifiably be believed very likely to possess. It is not very clear whether any
correspondence relation underlies or constitutes this 'truth':
sometimes 'facts' are introduced into the discussion. But in
any case an endless supply of propositions runs in our heads
or drops from our lips or flows from our pens; and these
abide our question. We talk, and logical positivism will tell

---

[1] For a criticism of the two general types of theory outlined in this section,
see Joachim, *The Nature of Truth*, chs. i and ii.

[2] Modern realism and logical positivism in their metaphysical attitude (or
in the latter case attitude towards metaphysics) reproduce in a mutilated form
the philosophical positions of Locke and Hume respectively.

us what we have meant—if we have meant anything. Only on propositions need the philosophic logician concentrate his attention. Analysed by a technique of symbols they will yield in terms of themselves the solutions of our logico-philosophical problems.

3. These types of theory are distinctive of the modern revolt from idealism. But they represent a general attitude common also to the eighteenth-century empiricism against which Hegel's criticism and construction were in part directed, and to the views which the British idealists of the nineteenth century set out to combat.[1]

Hence, and because the British idealists, though heirs of Hegel, have been less thoroughgoing in their idealism than he,[2] it will perhaps be not inappropriate to reverse historical order, and sketch their notion of truth as a stage intermediate between the theories outlined in the last section and Hegel's own more far-reaching doctrine. I have, indeed, already committed myself to this policy, particularly in Chapter X, §§ 4 ff., where I have freely borrowed from the teaching of F. H. Bradley and Bosanquet in discussing empirical thought and in criticizing logical theory which retains inflexibly the attitude of the Understanding. I will confine myself to the views of Bradley.   .

4. In 1883 Bradley conceived logic and psychology as two special sciences to be kept separate from one another and from metaphysics, and he did not at any time openly modify this position.[3] His division between logic and psychology is based upon a difference of 'aspect' in 'ideas'. Idea is (1) an immediate psychical fact, or mental image. It is an event occurring as a phase in the series of events or facts which constitutes the psychical history of this or that individual mind. This psychical process is the subject-matter of a special science of phenomenalist psychology, which studies the laws of coexistence and sequence governing these events;

---

[1] Coupled in the case of logical positivism with a respect for mathematics which has not been a common feature of British empiricism.

[2] See *Preface*, pp. xvi and xvii.

[3] What follows is in the main reproduced from parts II and III of an article entitled 'The Marriage of Universals', *Journal of Philosophical Studies* (now *Philosophy*), 1928, nos. 11 and 12.

and for such a science the individual mind is a 'soul'. But idea is (2) meaning. It is an ideal content which in the act of judgement is loosened from its existence or occurrence as a merely immediate psychical fact or event, and referred away as a universal to qualify the real. Idea in the second 'aspect' relates to idea in the first as symbolized to symbol, and only with idea in the second 'aspect' has logic any concern. For logic must study judgement as essentially a claim to assert truth, and only universal ideas in their reference to reality can be true or false.

4·1. Though the first chapter of Bradley's *Logic*, in which this theory of judgement is set forth, shows evident traces of Hegel's *Phänomenologie*, the doctrine at first sight closely resembles any empiricist theory of knowledge for which truth depends somehow on correspondence of a private mental image with an 'external' real, and thinking is taken to be essentially adjectival to a singular individual mind. The symbolic psychical fact looks like a go-between which copies and represents the real. We are then tempted to raise, as Cook Wilson did raise, the stock objection to any representative theory of cognition; urging that if this loosening of ideal content from psychical image falls within the judgement—if, i.e., the relation of symbol to symbolized is *for* the judging subject—then the psychical image becomes a part of the object of judgement, a part of the real to which the judgement is an act of reference. It would then presumably require a further image in order to be known, and so *ad infinitum*.[1]

4·2. But Bradley did not hold the representative doctrine of ideas, and this criticism misses much that is vital to his theory. At the risk of erring in the opposite direction we may construe his meaning differently. In the first place, the relation of symbol and symbolized holds not between idea as universal content, or universal meaning, and the real to which it is referred, but between idea as psychical image and idea as universal meaning. The real, that is to say, is not

---

[1] Or the objection may be put as a dilemma: Unless it is presupposed that I know both mental image and 'real' original, how can I know anything but the 'image'? If this *is* presupposed, on what grounds do I assert the relation of image and original as holding between them?

symbolized and meant by idea *qua* meaning: idea *qua* meaning is meant and symbolized by idea *qua* image. For Bradley's universal idea is not that secondary, derivative, product of an abstractive generalizing activity which on a consistent empiricist view the universal idea must become— although on such a view this 'activity' could be nothing but capricious distortion. Though Bradley may call the universal idea 'a part cut off' and referred away to reality, yet it is for him the essence of that from which it is cut off, or emerges 'loosened'; it is the mediate significance and real nature of the immediate psychical fact. Nor, on the other hand, is the subject-matter of phenomenalist psychology a residual 'part'—the empty eggshell from which ideal content has broken and flown: it is the whole experience viewed under a limited abstract 'aspect' as psychical process of immediate facts or events, the same whole experience which the logician views under a complementary abstract 'aspect' as mediate ideal content.

4·3. In the second place Bradley in 1908 owned himself guilty in his Logic at least of misleading language. He expressly asserted (*a*) that the idea (*qua* ideal content) cannot, as his words might have suggested, float loose in the mind, waiting to be referred in judgement to the real; and (*b*) that the recognized individual existence of the idea as symbol may be absent in the act of judgement, and must be ignored by the logician.[1]

This denial of floating ideas is of vital importance. Bradley confesses that he was formerly drawn to it by difficulties concerned with false and imaginary ideas, and with apparent suspension of judgement. He proceeds to show that any idea which we might suppose merely to float is already, in being entertained at all, asserted to exist in some not unreal world. In this rejection of floating ideas Bradley turns his back on the Cartesian theory of apprehension and judgement and on Kant's doctrine of free imagination as wholly unobjective, a doctrine which vitiates Kant's attack on the ontological argument and precludes Kant from any satisfactory treatment of the emotive states of the finite self. The

---

[1] See *Essays on Truth and Reality*, pp. 28 ff. In effect floating ideas are denied in *Appearance and Reality*, ch. xxiv.

doctrine is not consistent with that identity of content in the subjective and objective aspects of phenomena on which Kant's proof of the Analogies depends, but it is consistent with Kant's ascription of intuition to sense and not to thought, and with his consequent denial of self-transcendence in finite experience[1] and of degrees of reality.[2] On the other hand, it is utterly incompatible with Bradley's teaching that finite experience is self-transcending and that truth and reality have degree.

4·4. We may perhaps, then, discount Bradley's misleading metaphors and interpret him to mean that psychical fact and ideal content are two phases of one whole which develops. Moreover, since an image is clearly not something wholly immediate, we may suggest that Bradley's indiscriminate use of the terms 'image' and 'immediate fact' blurs two distinguishable phases of this development. We may suppose him to be introducing his conception of logic with a sketch of the development from sensuous immediacy through imagination to thought. So interpreted, Bradley would, I suppose, at the opening of his *Logic* be writing as a philosophical psychologist, or a philosopher of Spirit. His language would be neither that of logic nor that of a phenomenalist psychology, but would be admissible in the introductory chapters of a work devoted to either of these special sciences. It would recall Hegel's *Phänomenologie* and *Philosophie des Geistes*, from which much of it is, in fact, obviously derived.[3] *Appearance and Reality*, so far as it is constructive, might well be described as an effort to lay the foundation of such a philosophical psychology, or Philosophy of Spirit, by an Hegelian mistrustful of the dialectical method.

On the whole, that is, I think, a fair interpretation of Bradley's meaning. But it does not necessarily justify his view that immediate psychical fact and/or mental image can also be treated as events in temporal process by a phenomenalist psychology, nor does it fully explain the character of that special science of logic with which Bradley complements such a psychology. In particular, the relation for the

[1] See ch. ix, § 5.
[2] See ch. xii, § 2 *ad fin.*
[3] More remotely it would recall Aristotle's *De Anima*.

logician of ideal content to reality is as yet unclear. It is this
which we have now to examine.

4·5. The real to which ideal content is in judgement referred 'away' is a subject other than the existent psychical
fact from which it has been loosened. This subject is (*a*)
ultimately the Absolute; but (*b*) *qua* immediate (limited)
subject it is reality as 'presented' or 'given' within the context of the judgement. In thinking—at any rate as the
logician sees it—this limited subject expands as a coherently
developing system of ideal content. The relation, that is to
say, between ideal content and the real to which it has been
said by Bradley to be 'referred away' is no more that of copy
to independently existing 'realistic' original than was the
relation between psychical image and idea as ideal content.
The ideal content of judgement is (1) the genuine development of the content which in psychical fact was one with its
existence; but (2)—the second stage of the development—
it further turns out to be the content of, and so far one with,
the real to which it is 'referred'. For the real, in so far as it is
thought, *is* the ideal. Truth, accordingly, is not merely
dependent upon, or in any sense other than, the coherence
and comprehensiveness of systematically developing ideal
content: it *is* this developing system. 'Truth', says Bradley,
'is the whole Universe realizing itself in one aspect.'[1]

4·51. And so we find ourselves in effect asserting that
our thought is an activity of the real, its self-expression in
and as the finite thinking subject—a conception neither
empiricist nor Kantian and not far from Hegel's account in
the *Philosophy of Spirit* of Thinking as a phase of Concrete
Spirit.[2]

But though as a metaphysician Bradley does so regard
thinking, he conceives it the business of the logician to work
blinkered to this metaphysical truth. As on the one side the
logician must ignore the psychical aspect of idea, so on the

---

[1] *Essays on Truth and Reality*, p. 116. Cf. ibid., p. 114: 'The end of
truth is to be and to possess reality in an ideal form.' So to Aquinas truth is
'Being *qua* known', a doctrine which descends (through Aristotle) from Plato's
ἀλήθεια. On the union of coherence and comprehensiveness, and their
inclusion of the principle of non-contradiction, within system as the criterion
of truth, see ibid., ch. viii.

[2] Cf. *Enc.*, §§ 465–8; also ibid., § 415.

other he must leave merely implicit the ultimate relation of ideal content to reality.

4·6. Bradley's position now becomes difficult to define with confidence. For the moment let us borrow the logician's blinkers and try to make out what remains within his limited field of vision.

The immediate 'given' subject of judgement develops as an expanding ideal content; grows as a coherence of universal necessary connexions. But for two reasons this developing truth remains defective in principle. In the first place it cannot become complete truth until it embrace the Absolute, until no distinction remain between immediate and ultimate subject. Pending the fulfilment of this condition—which it cannot fulfil—it continues to be partially self-contradictory and incoherent because still in part determined from without itself, and it fails accordingly to be all-comprehensive. It is not, and it cannot be, fully systematic.[1] Secondly, it remains always untrue because it cannot contain within itself the psychological conditions of the act of judgement; it must pay for that abstraction from psychical fact upon which its status depends.

4·61. It would appear to follow that the blinkered logician is aware of psychical fact as the immediate subject of judgement; but inasmuch as this is immediate it is ineffable, and it may therefore, as it would seem, count as invisible. All he sees and can explain is a purely discursive mediation in terms of ideal content which is universal in the sense of wholly general and unindividual; an analytic dissolution wherein there is no reconstruction, even partial, of the 'real given in experience', i.e. no re-immediation, even provisional and insecure, of the immediate fact which served the mediating process for a starting-point. Though the spring of this process is the discrepancy (to use Bradley's terminology) of the 'what' with the 'that', which thinking strives to heal, yet for the logician this discrepancy is not *as such* present in thought; it is only reflected somehow in the endless unsatisfied expansion of unindividually universal ideal content.

4·7. This conception of thought is far more reminiscent

[1] See note on § 4·5 above.

of Kant than of Hegel. Bradley, like Kant, regards logic as primarily a theory of the judgement. The inevitable exclusion from ideal content of the psychological conditions of the act of judgement recalls Kant's severance of his wholly non-intuitive Understanding from sense; and when Bradley stigmatizes this exclusion as 'failure', we are reminded of Kant's relapse into empiricism, his view of the object of knowledge as a *quasi*-whole of merely possible experience radiating out from an actual focus of immediate sensuous intuition.[1] Again, the indefinitely regressive *ab extra* necessitation which systematizes Kant's phenomenal world seems to be reproduced in the endless expansion of Bradley's ideal content. The Bradleian logician must treat thought as purely discursive, and the account which he must give of thought would not seem greatly to conflict with Kant's view that man's knowing, his true and objective thinking, is typified *par excellence* by physical theory. In this expansion of ideal content the Bradleian Absolute seems as remote and unknown as the Kantian thing-in-itself, the criterion of systematic totality as dim and uncomprehended in its operation as the purely regulative Kantian Idea of the unconditioned.

4·8. If this conception of thinking[2] is pressed, it turns out to be nonsense. Such a purely discursive, purely centrifugal radiation of universal character—of 'what' divorced from 'that'—would be not expansion but dispersion, not development but incontinent self-dissolution. If thought has for its function such sheer discursion, unpunctuated by any phase of re-immediation, then its task of achieving truth as system is not merely fated to fail of final accomplishment; it cannot begin. A logic constructed upon such an hypothesis is open to all the objections which were urged against Kant's view of thought as a wholly unintuitive function in which Reason plays no constitutive role.[3] It would be less even than a logic of sheer validity.[4]

---

[1] Cf. ch. ix, §§ 4·31 and 4·311 above.
[2] Which, so far as I can judge, is the logical theory attributed to Bradley by Mr. Morris in chapters viii and ix of his *Idealistic Logic*.
[3] See esp. ch. ix, § 4·3 above.
[4] A psychology constructed on the hypothesis of psychical facts construed

5. Yet Bradley conceives finite experience as essentially self-transcending, and repudiates the floating idea. He allows that the universal even for logic is concrete, in itself identity in difference and not, as in effect it is for Kant, merely synthesized as a severality of concepts which meet in the singular sense-intuition.

We must, then, attempt to interpret Bradley's *Logic* by the best in it and not the worst. There is an important passage in which the logician's field of vision is momentarily widened, and he is permitted to recognize his criterion of truth for what it is.

'What was it', Bradley asks,[1] 'that guided our half-conscious thoughts, and forced us to see failure where we desired success? To perceive imperfection is to judge by the perfect, and we wish to become aware of this idea which has served us as a canon and touchstone of reason.'

On the following page comes the reply:

'There has come in to us here, shut up within these poor logical confines, and pondering on the union of two abstract functions, a vision of absolute consummation. In this identity of analysis and synthesis we recognize an appearance of our soul's ideal . . . which . . . is at bottom the notion of a perfected individuality.'

Perfected individuality means to Bradley all-comprehensive totality actively self-determining in and through coherent elements which suffer no unresolved mutual contradiction, present no opaque residue which remains unabsorbed within the system; for elsewhere Bradley says, 'there is nothing which, to speak properly, is individual or perfect, except only the Absolute'.[2] Truth, in short, is system; and system is nothing static, but the activity which Absolute Experience is. We might suppose that in the light of this vision the logician would be permitted henceforth to work openly with this criterion of perfected individuality.

5·1. But he is not. Bradley's account of inference shows

as events would be equally bankrupt. In Part II of the article referred to in note on § 4 I have tried to show that Bradley's phenomenalist psychology only works by means of the surreptitious re-introduction of that aspect of idea which he has officially excluded from psychology and assigned to logic.

[1] Ed. 2, p. 489.
[2] *Appearance & Reality*, ed. 2, p. 217.

him still in two minds. He clings to the Kantian view that logic is primarily concerned with the judgement, yet he holds that judgement unmediated is nothing, and that judgement is everywhere inference, though not explicitly inference, and though differing from inference in form. Inference he defines as 'the ideal self-development of an object',[1] but throughout the last two chapters of his Logic and the first Terminal Essay of the second edition he dwells on the impossibility for logic of reconciling within inference the inferring subject's partly arbitrary activity with the necessity wherewith conclusion must flow from premisses. That somehow these conflicting factors are two sides of a joint activity[2] must, as it seems, remain for logic a postulate to be justified only in metaphysics.

5·2. When we leave the blinkered logician and pass the barrier which Bradley declines to abolish, we expect to meet the metaphysician awaiting us on the other side with a fuller interpretation of truth as system. Surely we shall find that with him the passing glimpse has become an abiding illumination. Surely he will show us truth as the systematic activity of an Absolute that is nothing but truth.

But we are disappointed. Bradley declines to follow Hegel in identifying Absolute Experience with thought, regarding it instead as that into which thought must of its own nature strive to pass, but can pass—if that is passing—only by an act of suicide. For thought is, even from a metaphysical standpoint, only mediate and discursive. It spins its web of relations which are—self-contradictorily and beyond hope of reconciliation—both internal and external. This relational form can never express a perfectly individual system, and it is only a makeshift *modus vivendi*; but we cannot transcend it and still think. The Absolute, the perfect individual, is not thought but immediate feeling above mediation; its form is supra-relational.

Thus we do not pass in metaphysics beyond the same bewildering paradox which met us in logic. Truth is system, and system is individuality. Yet, while only thinking can be true, the only perfect individual is the Absolute, and Absolute Experience is not thought.

[1] *Logic*, ed. 2, p. 597.   [2] Ibid., p. 592, note 5.

5.3. It may well seem that Bradley's metaphysical conclusions, like Kant's, must render impossible the reasoning
which is claimed to lead up to them. But we are concerned
not with the difficulties in Bradley's conception of Absolute
Experience, but in making a just estimate of what on the
whole was his conception of truth.

A comprehensive study of his work shows, I think, that
the view of thought as purely discursive, which I have called
nonsensical if pressed, was never held by Bradley. His
insistence even as a logician upon the principle of identity in
difference and the concrete universal, his confession that
even in logic the activity of the Real in judgement and inference must be recognized, leave no doubt that for Bradley
truth meant not static coherence but self-developing system:
system within which comprehensiveness and coherence are
moments of an activity which is the activity of the Absolute,
however much more than that activity the Absolute may be
—however far on Bradley's view, that is to say, truth may
fall short of Reality. If we contrive to think ourselves into
the historical context in which Bradley's logical theory
matured; if we make due allowance for Bradley's desire not
indeed to compromise but to accept battle on his opponents'
ground and show the germ of rationality in common-sense
empirical thinking;[1] then we can come to no other conclusion. And our further corollary must be that, although
Bradley as a metaphysician will not have it that Absolute
experience is thought, yet his logic clearly fails to work
without metaphysic, and he would have done better to confess it a metaphysical inquiry.

6.[2] The undeniable ambiguity in Bradley's position
scarcely excuses, although it partly explains, the degree of
misinterpretation which the logic of idealism has in recent
years suffered even from sympathetic critics. Mr. C. R.
Morris, for example, in his *Idealistic Logic* (1) regards the
'coherence theory' of truth as post-Bradleian; (2) excludes

---

[1] Cf. *Logic*, ed. 2, p. 583: 'If we mean to keep to a view of reality which
is anything like our common ideas (and apart from a system of metaphysics
we cannot, I think, do anything else) . . .'.

[2] The reader not specially interested in British philosophy is recommended
to omit the rest of this chapter except §§ 7–7.3.

comprehensiveness from the criterion of truth which he supposes that theory to maintain; (3) appears to assume that truth on that theory belongs to a static linkage of judgements which are corrigible by a singular judging subject, but are not necessarily maintained by the coherence theory to be the phases of a *self*-developing activity which works jointly in the finite judging subject and his object.

A glance at Bradley's *Principles of Logic*, ed. 2, p. 620, will show that (1) and (2) are not historically correct. (3), even if it be a possible inference from isolated passages in Bradley, is the merest travesty of idealist logic because it flatly ignores the original unity of thought and being without which idealism cannot stand at all. A logic thus emasculated is mere Protagoreanism: truth, developing under purely subjective correction, becomes a fabrication which neither depends on correspondence to the real, nor is coherence of the real. However strictly Bradley tried to bound logic, he was not a formal logician deluded by the belief that logical and metaphysical theory can vary quite independently of one another. He may use the terms 'existence' and 'reality' ambiguously, but he never in logic maintained degrees of truth without degrees of reality. He calls thought essentially discursive, but he rejects the doctrine of floating ideas. It is mere caricature to depict him as in effect confining man's knowledge of the individual to awareness of existence given in sense-intuition without mode or degree. Mr. Morris did a service by bringing out the closeness of Bradley to Kant, but even the limited scope of his work is hardly an excuse for playing Hamlet quite without the Prince. Bradley rejected a dialectical logic of categories, but his Logic is not fully intelligible without Hegel's *Phänomenologie* and *Philosophie des Geistes*, and much of it might be called a small-scale application of the teaching of Hegel's Logic.

6·1. Dr. Ewing's criticism of the coherence theory in *Idealism*, chapter v, is careful and sympathetic. He reminds us more than once that to Bradley nothing is real but experience. Yet he tends in general to sever 'epistemological' from metaphysical arguments for idealism in a manner which no idealist holding a coherence doctrine of truth could tolerate, and he quite fails to see the central importance of

Bradley's view that degrees of reality are the inseparable counterpart to degrees of truth. That the real is *operative* in judgement is surely a tenet common to all the post-Hegelian British idealists whom Dr. Ewing considers—certainly to Green, Caird, Bradley, Bosanquet, and Joachim. But Dr. Ewing, convinced that 'cognition is rather of the nature of finding than making', declines to see in the idealist usage of 'construction' any sense but that of practical making.[1] Yet I can think of no British idealist who did not, like Bradley, mean by it a joint activity of the judging subject and of the real: 'construction' in idealist doctrine is as much a constructing of the thinker as of the object thought. I can see no reason why to call cognition 'constructive' should any more imply confusion with practice than to term aesthetic activity 'creative'. I doubt if Dr. Ewing realizes quite how far from idealism his own doctrine is. To regard cognition as mere finding can only lead to sheer empiricism, with its inevitable consequence that by thinking we cannot learn— indeed can only distort our passively accepted data.

6·2. When Professor H. H. Price in his inaugural lecture on *Truth and Corrigibility* abstracts corrigibility as an arguable doctrine held in common by certain idealists and certain logical positivists, he is deluded by what is practically an equivocal term. No idealist could hold such a doctrine as he outlines. 'Corrigibility', it must be admitted, was not a fortunate term for idealists to select. It is apt to suggest— and evidently has suggested—if not adjustment by means of a measuring instrument, at any rate the reshaping of an artefact which remains relatively external to the activity producing it.[2] It hints at flirtation with the fallacy of treating thought as a technique, and at a latent hankering after a correspondence test of truth. When logicians of the Understanding combine it with a notion of static coherence, the result is a sort of Chinese puzzle theory. Thinking is made to consist in the putting together of pieces which nearly fit in several ways, but not perfectly save in one.

6·3. The complete *ignoratio elenchi* betrayed by these

---

[1] Compare also Professor H. A. Prichard, *Kant's Theory of Knowledge*, p. 118.

[2] Cf. ch. ii, § 5·2 above.

efforts to appraise idealist doctrines as if they were undenominational gives one to think. The later Scholastics
studied Aristotle industriously enough, but they became
gradually numb to the meaning of what they read. From
their time to that of Hegel, Greek philosophy passed through
perversion to neglect. One wonders whether, at least in this
country, the idealism in which Greek speculation was reborn
has begun to suffer a similar fate. There are signs, at any
rate among our professional thinkers, of an analogous in-
ability to grasp even the bare meaning of an idealist philosophy—signs which are least mistakable when the criticism
directed against idealism is at once uncomprehending and
tolerant. Idealism is little helped by critics who take up the
general attitude that provided idealists will not insist too
strongly that 'correction' entails a thorough modification of
the old pieces of the puzzle, and provided they will not press
their absurd, or at least quite unwarranted assertion that the
universe is all one puzzle, then there may be something in
the coherence theory of truth. When an idealist is in effect
told that if he will stop talking of self-development, and at
least drop the capital W when he speaks in print of the
Whole, he may come tolerably near to British common
sense, he will do well to fear Danaan gifts. It may be that in
this and some other countries the main impulse of European
speculation is destined to sterility for a time, but if compromise mate with sympathetic misinterpretation their issue
can only be cretinous.

7. We have been led into a difficult discussion. I will end
it by trying to point out the main issue plainly.

From Hegel's point of view the question to be asked of
all the thinkers whom I have roughly classed as logicians
of the Understanding are these. 'You offer', Hegel might
say to each of them, 'an account of thought and truth which
you regard as at any rate applicable to everyday empirical
thinking and to the thinking of special science. Do you
(*a*) further hold that the nature of thought and knowledge
has everywhere sufficient sameness to justify you in extend-
ing your logical theory to cover all thinking? Or do you
(*b*) hold that there are grades of thinking and degrees of
truth? And if you embrace the latter alternative, how does

it affect your attitude to the lower-grade thinking of common sense and special science?'

7·1. The realist, the traditional formal logician, and the logical positivist would presumably at once accept the first alternative, and enough has been said to indicate the line that Hegel's criticism would then take. Kant would claim to have supplemented formal with transcendental logic so as to cover at any rate all thinking which is also the knowing of an object; and again the outline of Hegel's retort has been given: What kind of thinking, then, is Kant's own critical thinking?

7·2. Bradley would have agreed that there are grades of thinking and degrees of truth, and he would presumably have pointed out that in discussing low-grade thinking his intention never was to take it simply as it stands, as *reell* in Hegel's sense of the word. Bradley was not merely offering a natural history of thought, but attempting always to display low-grade thinking as a germ developing itself towards a higher form of experience, transcending itself in the light of a criterion of system which operates in it and moves it as a final cause. He would therefore have disagreed totally with the realists and with the formal logicians old and new, because, he would have said, low-grade thinking *wie es geht und steht* is not what it is when seen in the light of what it strives towards. All that lives, *a fortiori* thought, is self-transcending, and low-grade thinking, as it stands, matters only to the low-grade thinker. So far he would have accepted Hegel's notion of philosophic interpretation, and even have permitted himself to use it in logic.

Hegel might then, I think, have replied: 'If you accept my principle of philosophic interpretation, on the strength of what other principle do you stop half-way and maintain that thought is purely discursive and passes into a higher form of experience by suicide? Your position, if pressed, turns out to be not that thought is from the beginning of its development the germ of a higher form of experience than thought, but that thought has in it from birth the germ of a deadly disease, the seed of a mortal despair—or rather that thought is by its very destiny stillborn. You find cold and ghost-like the notion that reality could be the same as under-

standing, and your words betray you as after all, like Kant,
a logician of the mere Understanding. Nor is it any wonder
that when you turn metaphysician, some call you mystic,
others sceptic.'

7·3. Yet that would not have been Hegel's last word. It
is well to press any philosophical position to its logical conclusion, but that pressure yields only a half truth. In
Aristotle, Spinoza, Kant, and Bradley alike the interest
lies precisely in the difference and the conflict between what
their thought is as it stands and the nature it is striving to
fulfil. This is the only philosophic interest, and it operates
on the same principle when we reflect on empirical thinking,
and when we study the writings of any individual philosopher.[1] That is the lesson of development which Hegel
learnt in the first instance from Aristotle and himself developed, and he vindicated it perhaps more triumphantly
in the history of philosophy than in any other sphere.
Though Bradley came after Hegel, and without Hegel is not
intelligible, yet we cannot in judging him ignore the context
of backward British philosophy in which he played the part
of a reformer.

8. Bernard Bosanquet was a more constant student of
Hegel than Bradley. He shared Bradley's conception of
logic as a special science, and a comparison of their *Logics*
does not seem to show any marked difference of position.
On the other hand, in his Gifford Lectures, *The Principle of
Individuality and Value* and *The Value and Destiny of the
Individual*, Bosanquet adopts a somewhat different attitude.
His effort to show the essential and constitutive rationality
in all the higher forms of experience, and everywhere to
identify truth as system with individuality, suggest a total
breach with Kant and a conception of true thinking much
nearer to Hegel than to Bradley. But neither in his Gifford
Lectures nor in any later work did Bosanquet take the de-
cisive step of throwing down the Bradleian barrier between
logic and metaphysics. The biological sub-title of his *Logic*—
The Morphology of Knowledge—indicates that he is trying to
elicit the structure of thought in its phenomenal embodiment

[1] Cf. EL, § 22, *Zusatz*: 'The business of philosophy is only to bring into
explicit consciousness what the world in all ages has believed about thought.'

(of empirical thinking) rather than to display the phases of its pure activity. To Bosanquet as a logician the activity of thought means essentially an activity centred in, though doubtless also transcending, the finite individual thinker. But just so far as activity is finite and imperfect, it issues in a product which falls in some measure outside it. The elements comprising Bosanquet's morphological structure, the affiliated forms of judgement and argument which he tabulates,[1] inevitably appear rather as characters which classify products of thought than as integral phases in the activity of thought itself. They are, in Gentile's terminology, forms rather of *pensiero pensato* than of *pensiero pensante*. Bosanquet's *Logic* is still, like Bradley's, only one stage beyond what Hegel calls a natural history of thought.

His final position is ambiguous. In *Implication and Linear Inference*, ch. v, he appears to assume that to elaborate a dialectical logic of categories is a legitimate philosophical industry, but throughout the book his constructive doctrine is based upon his usual courteous criticism of logicians of the Understanding, and it does not rise very high above this foundation. He does in a footnote on p. 95 touch sympathetically on the suggestion that all judgements are in some degree judgements of value, but the implication of his treatment of the concrete universal in the Gifford Lectures is not fully elaborated.

[1] Ed. 2, vol. i, p. 86, and vol. ii, p. 39.

XIV

HEGEL'S CONCEPTION OF TRUTH

1. THE previous chapter has to some extent prepared us for
the distinction which Hegel draws between truth in a philosophic sense (*Wahrheit*) and correctness (*Richtigkeit*).[1] These
terms, as he says, are often treated as synonymous in common
life, but truth in the sense of correctness means

'merely the agreement of an object with our conception (*Vorstellung*)
of it. We thus presuppose an object to which our conception must
conform. In the philosophical sense of the word, on the other hand,
truth may be described in general abstract terms as the agreement of
a content (*Inhalt*) [*sc.* a thought-content] with itself. . . . The deeper
and philosophical meaning of truth can be partially traced in the
ordinary usage of language. Thus we speak of a true friend; by which
we mean a friend whose manner of conduct accords with the notion
(*Begriff*) of friendship. In the same way we speak of a true work of
art. Untrue in this sense means the same as bad or self-discordant.'[2]

2. In this account of truth two points are obvious. Truth
in the full sense of the word (*a*) belongs to the object, and
(*b*) is a value, a good. Hegel's *Wahrheit* is in these respects
the same as Plato's ἀλήθεια. When Hegel attributes the
value, or good, which truth is—'genuineness' might provisionally express it—to that which accords with its notion,
we are reminded of Plato's doctrine of definition in teleological terms in *Republic* 342e ff., and of the normative
aspect of the Platonic Forms, in particular of the Form of the
Good. We recall, too, the development of this doctrine in
Aristotle's conception of the natural specimen as an approximation definable only in terms of that specific form which is
its formal as well as final and efficient cause.[3] But though
Aristotle maintains the identity of fully actual thought with
its object, neither the Platonic Form nor the Aristotelian
form is quite explicitly expressed as being itself the activity

---

[1] But perhaps not entirely; see § 5 below.

[2] EL, § 24, *Zusatz* (2).

[3] Cf. ch. ii, §§ 2–5 above. For the relation of a thing to its notion, or ideal
norm, the Understanding substitutes its relation to an average, or at most to
an abstract type.

of thought. It is true that Aristotle's God is a thinking activity identical with the thinking which is its object, but Aristotle does not concentrate his whole philosophic effort upon exhibiting this identity of subject and object as the norm governing his *Scala Universi*, and to call his philosophy idealist is misleading. His substantial forms are still the real and intelligible rather than themselves thought, and his God is still substance.

2·1. This community of meaning in ἀλήθεια and *Wahrheit* is the thread of essential sameness which links Greek philosophy with modern idealism. It is the very nerve of that continuity which binds as phases in one development all philosophies which truly accord with the notion of philosophy.[1] But the conception of philosophic thinking as essentially awareness of value is explicit and central in Hegelianism as in Greek philosophy it never quite is. The point is not merely that Hegel, in holding truth to be a value or goodness in the object, did not conceive it as a character of a real which is presupposed as independent of thought— Plato himself had not presupposed any such independence, but had assumed, though naïvely, the kinship of mind with its object. But when Hegel says not only that truth is the accordance of an object with its notion, but also that it is the agreement of a content with itself, then he is conceiving reality no longer as mere intelligible substance-form but as itself active thought. The transition from substance to subject is made, and Hegel is saying that truth is value known so far as the knowing is explicit self-consciousness. Truth, he means, is a self-accordant thought-content, because in and as the object *qua* true the subject knows its own active self. To Hegel knowledge of value and knowledge of self are one and the same, and error is the belief that an object experienced as alien to the subject is, as so experienced, true in the philosophic sense of 'genuine'.

2·2. We may remark a corollary in passing. Despite the difference of explicit from implicit which distinguishes Hegel from the Greeks, his idealism is not reached by 'reifying' a thought-content already defined—as Descartes

[1] In British idealism its least ambiguous expression has been Bosanquet's Gifford Lectures; see ch. xiii, § 8 above.

defined thought—in opposition to the object of thought.[1]
He does not, like, e.g., Berkeley, come to idealism through
antithetic reaction from empirical realism. If we examine
Hegel's reasoning—particularly his not infrequent attacks
on subjective idealism—with the prepossession that Hegelian
idealism is merely one of two alternative 'epistemological'
theories as to how thought relates to its objects, we shall
probably get the impression that he is arguing not that only
thought is real, but that if and so far as reality is intelligible
it must itself be thought. But that prepossession will still
conceal from us Hegel's full meaning. For to Hegel the
problem is not how to patch up a relation between a thought
and a real object already fatally severed: on Hegel's view
the agreement of object with *Vorstellung*, which constitutes
the 'truth' of common life, is correspondence of his object
with the mere, still partly sensuous, idea of a singular experient.[2] The problem for Hegel is how to show the
apparent severance between thought and its object as in the
last resort necessitated by their real identity. And that is
why Hegel sees in idealism the inevitable development from
the fulness and balance of classical Greek philosophy, which
no intervening thinker ever quite reproduced.

3. Hegel's conception, then, of truth as self-accordance,
the accordance of anything with its real nature, its notion,
entails the view that reality and thought, in the fullest sense
of each, are one and the same. It can hardly become clear
until we have studied the logic of the Notion, but a criticism
of Kant which Hegel makes in LL ii, pp. 27–9, illustrates
it well enough to seem worth quoting at length, even at the
risk of anticipating a not fully established doctrine.

3·1. In KRV, B, p. 82, Kant grants, regarding it as trivial
(a mere verbal definition), the description of truth as correspondence of knowledge with its object. This Hegel calls
a most valuable definition of truth.[3] Yet, he observes, it is
a fundamental principle of Kant's transcendental idealism
that reality, things as they really are in themselves, cannot
be comprehended by rational cognition, but lie quite outside

---

[1] Cf. ch. x, § 2·1 above.
[2] This is the normal meaning of *Vorstellung* in Hegel.
[3] *Sc.* if properly interpreted as self-accordance.

the notion (*Begriff*).[1] Hence it is obvious that a Reason of this sort which can establish no correspondence between itself and its object (things-in-themselves), and things-in-themselves which do not correspond with the notion, are two equally untrue presentations (*Vorstellungen*). Thus Kant, rejecting as he does the conception of an intuitive Understanding, fails after all to make truth the correspondence of knowledge with its object.

3·2. Hegel then summarizes Kant's further statements to this effect: People demand to know a universal and safe criterion of the truth of every cognition. This would be a criterion of every cognition without distinction of object. But abstraction is here made from every content of cognition (i.e. from every relation of cognition to its object). But truth is concerned precisely with this content. Hence it would be quite impossible and absurd to ask for a mark of the truth of this content of cognitions.

'Here', comments Hegel, 'the common view (*Vorstellung*) of the formal function of logic is very definitely expressed, and the argument quoted appears very enlightening. But to begin with it must be observed that such formal argumentation commonly comes to forget, as it proceeds, the matter (*die Sache*) which it has made its foundation and is now discussing. It would be absurd, we are told, to demand a criterion of the truth of the content of cognition. But, according to the definition, it is not the content which constitutes truth, but its correspondence with the *Begriff*. A content devoid of the *Begriff*, such as Kant here speaks of, is something notionless and therefore without essence. Of course it is impossible to demand a criterion of the truth of such a thing, but for the opposite reason, namely because, being a notionless content, it is not the requisite correspondence and can be no more than something which belongs to truthless opinion.[2]

---

[1] Hegel's language is not perfectly clear. He means that on Kant's view the Ideas of Reason are merely regulative and constitute no object, while the categories, the pure *Begriffe*, constitute a merely phenomenal object.

[2] In accepting as valuable the definition of truth as correspondence Hegel is interpreting it to mean not that truth is correspondence of knowledge with an object independent of mind (not, i.e., correspondence in the sense indicated in ch. xiii, §§ 2 and 2·1), but that truth is the whole concrete of knowing and known in relation. The term 'content' then means the object *qua* the 'filling' of the cognition. Kant, Hegel is maintaining, has accepted the definition in this same sense when he explains the 'content' of cognition as the relation of cognition to its object, and says that truth is concerned precisely with that

'It is the content which here causes the confusion—a confusion which on all occasions besets formalism, and compels it to say the opposite of what it intends to put forward whenever it attempts explanation. Suppose, then, that we ignore the content and halt at the abstract view that the logical is merely formal and abstracts from all content. But if we do that we are left with a one-sided cognition which is to contain no object, an empty indeterminate form which is neither correspondence (since correspondence demands two terms) nor truth. In the *a priori* synthesis of the *Begriff* Kant had a higher principle. In that principle the demand of truth could be satisfied: duality could be cognized in unity. But the sense-material, the manifold of intuition, had too much hold upon him. He could not leave it and treat the *Begriff*[1] and the categories *in and for themselves*, and so achieve a speculative method in philosophy.'

4. Hegel says also that *das Wahre ist das Ganze*. He does not mean by *das Ganze* a whole which consists of one total interconnected object conceived realistically as indifferent to its coming to be object; nor does he mean a whole consisting in one all-embracing complex of propositions correctly corresponding to such a total object. He means that truth is the 'genuineness' of one spiritual activity of knowing, whose knowing is self-knowing. The whole which truth is, is the totality of phases in that self-knowing activity which, as has been said before, is the subject's self-diremption and reunion with itself. Truth to Hegel is *one* coherence, or self-accordance, only because spirit is one in the diversity

content. But Kant is, Hegel thinks, at the same time and contradictorily taking 'content' to be something which resides in a diversity of objects 'detached' from the cognition of them (i.e. interpreting correspondence in the sense of ch. xiii, §§ 2 and 2·1). With this latter interpretation in mind, Kant rejects the demand for a universal criterion of truth on the implied ground that only in actual cognition can you reach these diverse 'contents', and that an *a priori* test of the truth of actual cognitions is impossible. Hegel retorts that such 'contents' detached from thought have no essence, i.e. no objective existence at all. There is certainly no criterion of their truth; but that is because they are mere contents of arbitrary subjective opinion, not because you cannot reach them, get into touch with them, save in the act of cognition. KRV, B, pp. 235–6, well illustrates the difficulty in Kant's phenomenalism.

[1] Throughout the whole passage cited Hegel seems to be using the term *Begriff* with reference to Kant to mean the whole conceptual element involved in any cognition. In this sentence he appears to use it with special reference to the transcendental unity of apperception.

of all its phases.[1] A realist cannot logically—and commonly does not—assert monism. For of the unifying principles which the Understanding detects in its 'detached' object-world, not one is adequate to unify that world as a single whole. Kant took the first step towards objective idealism by interpreting necessity as the mind's imposition, and exalting some of these unifying principles to the status of categories. Kant's categories do claim to express the objective world as a single whole, but only in the patently half-way shape of indefinite regress. On Hegel's view only subject—not substance, nor cause, nor even reciprocity—can truly claim to unify the world as a single whole. Hegel's monism is an effort to display as one concrete self-developing system the unity of the subject in all experience. Kant, denying to man at once any speculative knowledge of values and any concrete self-consciousness, could only adumbrate that unity in his doctrines of (a) the transcendental unity of apperception as an abstract subject, posited as spontaneously active, but functioning through categories not seriously deduced, either in their mutual connexion or in their connexion with the subject, and of (b) the purely regulative function of the Ideas of speculative Reason.

5. In this *Introduction* I have in the main tried to prepare the way for Hegel's conception of philosophic truth by treating my theme in what the ordinary logician would call 'logical' terms. I have chiefly occupied the reader's attention with the contrast which Hegel draws between the correct thinking of the Understanding and the 'genuine' thought of Reason. In particular, I have emphasized against formal logic, against Kant, and to a much lesser extent against Bradley, the Hegelian view that thought is in its own nature intuitive.

In so doing I have not put forward the whole of Hegel's case; or at least I have left one-half of it inadequately developed. I can well imagine even a not wholly unsym-

---

[1] Cf. EL, § 83, *Zusatz*: 'Truth as such must verify *itself*. Here, within the sphere of logic, this verification is given when the Notion demonstrates itself to be what is mediated through and with itself, and thus at the same time to be truly immediate.'

[2] Cf. ch. ix, § 4·1 above.

pathetic reader still shocked by this doctrine that truth is knowledge of value, or good, which is self-consciousness. I fancy that he may still object that such teaching permits the intrusion of feeling into thought; flirts with some such sentimentalism as Matthew Arnold's definition of philosophy as 'science tinged with emotion'. He will say, perhaps, that so-called judgements of value entail emotional approval or disapproval, whereas thought, if its proper pursuit of truth is to be successful in *any* field, must work in indifference to emotion.

5·1. The position of such an objector has obvious difficulties of its own. (*a*) It may lead him towards saying that a judgement of value is nothing but a judgement about the purely subjective emotional state of the experient; that it merely states the fact that the experient has certain feelings, and asserts no character in any other object. If so, his conclusion will shock most intelligent men, and it will lay on him the onus of producing a psychological doctrine to account for the odd contradiction of a purely emotional 'judgement'. He will not find it easy to explain how it is that we judge truth itself a value, or a good, and he will soon be in danger of lapsing into a purely physiological behaviourism. Or (*b*), in fear of this fate, he may boldly assert that goodness of this kind or of that is a character, particular, or, maybe, 'toti-resultant', which is simply recognized as belonging to a 'detached' real.

Of these two theories of value, the former provokes the retort: 'How, then, can *our* emotions matter?' To the latter we can only answer: 'Why, then, should goodness matter to *us*?' Nevertheless, I doubt if the reader will be satisfied with Hegel's position as I have so far shown it. He will still in all likelihood insist that thought, in order to reach truth, must be 'cool' and unbiased by emotion. I think I cannot better conclude this *Introduction* than by trying to expand that side of Hegel's case on which I touched in Chapter VIII, although nothing but the detailed study of the *Philosophy of Spirit* can really supply what lacks. I can only speak very roughly.

5·2. Hegel would agree that at any rate the Understanding properly exercised at its own level is unemotional. In this proper exercise the subject takes itself as 'detached' not merely from its object-world but also from any feelings in any way connected with that object. Pleasure and pain, desire and shrinking, hope and fear, are all there irrelevant. In mathematics, in natural science, and in the field of everyday empirical facts, to entertain these feelings for the cognized object itself is impossible or absurd, and to feel them in some more remote connexion with it can only distort or hinder the thinking of the Understanding.

But Understanding as a phase of Concrete Spirit has two 'aspects'. (*a*) For itself it is an intransigent repulsion of its 'detached' object-world. It reconstitutes the sensuously 'given' as a world without values which is emphatically not itself. So far as sense still remains for the Understanding an unabsorbed residue, that residue is merely opaque. That is to say, it is for the subject merely what he has failed to understand; it is not a residue of feeling.[1] But (*b*) the Understanding has constituted itself out of sensuous phases which form a developing series whose roots run through Soul and Nature down to Time and Space. Below Understanding sense is just as much self-feeling as it is feeling of not-self. It is only at the level of Understanding that we are so much occupied by the part which sensation plays in cognition of a 'detached' world that we think of a sense-content as nothing but a datum for the Understanding, a *sensum*; forgetting that it is also a feeling, or possesses, as it may be expressed in a metaphor borrowed from physics, an 'emotional charge'.

5.3. Thus, within the triad sense-Understanding-Reason we have so far mainly considered the relation between the antithesis and the synthesis, perhaps too much neglecting the triad as a whole.[2] We must now recollect that Understanding, as a level of Concrete Spirit, lies between two levels. Below it (to speak roughly and generally) is a felt oneness with what we scarcely sever from ourselves as an

[1] Because its object is to the Understanding only its *proximate* lower self; cf. ch. viii, § 3.12.
[2] Yet the reader will see that Hegel's definition of truth is, in effect, a short statement of his doctrine of philosophic interpretation; cf. ch. viii, above, esp. § 3.2.

object. No distinction between emotion and the cognition of a 'detached' world has yet emerged. Above it is the explicit consciousness of self in an object which therefore is not 'detached', and is apprehended in terms of value. This awareness of value is first practical: it begins in will. It develops through the aesthetic and the religious consciousness, and its highest form is philosophic knowledge.[1]

5·4. Hence the proper exercise of the Understanding is not emotional, nor is the rational experience of value emotional, if 'emotional' means depressed towards a level of blind feeling which belongs to spirit at a level of development lower even than Understanding.[2] But the experience of value does contain, sublated and made explicit, that intimate but blindly felt union of self and not-self which the Understanding arises to repudiate, but from which it sprang.

Moreover, the Understanding, like any dialectical antithesis, is a development of, not merely an opposite to, its thesis.[3] At the level of the Understanding the moment of feeling, or emotion, in all human experience is not quite simply discarded to be somehow held in total abeyance until a higher level is reached. If it were, it could never again

[1] I have here grouped all the forms of Concrete Spirit which express value, taking them together as a synthesis led up to by sense as thesis and Understanding as antithesis. I have thus departed from the letter of Hegel's *Philosophy of Spirit*, in which the main triad appears as Subjective Spirit, Objective Spirit, Absolute Spirit; cf. ch. viii, §§ 6–6·3 above. Hegel's triadic division marks the facts (*a*) that although Objective Spirit, the sphere of will, is awareness of value, it is not yet the explicit rational self-consciousness which Absolute Spirit is; and (*b*) that sense and Understanding are spirit considered subjectively as faculty, whereas at the practical levels of will spirit is objective in the sense that it begins to cancel its own 'detachment' from its object, and, in an antithetic phase, appropriate what had before seemed alien.

I think I have not falsified Hegel's teaching by this simplification, but I must add that in the *Philosophy of Spirit* 'Reason', *qua* a subjective faculty, appears immediately above Understanding. I have thus used the term 'Understanding' a little more broadly than does Hegel in that context, but not, I think, more broadly than Hegel uses it elsewhere.

These are points to be made clear in a detailed examination of the *Philosophy of Spirit*, which I cannot in this *Introduction* attempt.

[2] Depression of the experience of values to a lower form is, of course, not only possible but extremely common.

[3] See ch. xii, § 1·3 above.

become integral to experience. Because the original unity of thought and being persists unbroken, the subject in Understanding cannot be simply blind to the *existence* of feelings, any more than it can be simply blind to the existence of thoughts. We do and must attempt to produce empirical psychologies of the emotions—to 'understand' them—just as we do and must produce formal logics of thought. But when we do so, we can only make of the emotions 'valueless' things which appear part and parcel of the Understanding's 'detached' world of objects, and it is fatally easy for us then to forget the provisional hypothesis under which we work, and to assimilate the spiritual to the non-spiritual.

5·5. Finally, we may repeat again what was stated at greater length but with less ground in Chapter VIII, §§ 6·4– 6·43: If the experience of value does not culminate in the knowledge of truth, then the experience of good in conduct, and in aesthetic and religious consciousness, must remain unintelligible, and we have no right whatever to call moral, aesthetic, and religious experience a part of the heritage of man *qua* rational animal.

It is the eternal ironic paradox of human speculation that the more cautious philosophic doctrine ends always in an appeal to faith, which, if it be better than knowledge, is better only than the knowledge which the bare Understanding brings. When Kant makes amends for confining speculative knowledge to phenomenal objects by allowing that the Ideas of practical Reason do in some sense give knowledge in their regulation of conduct, as the Ideas of speculative Reason when they regulate the Understanding do not, he thinks to justify man's experience of value. But he cannot show that this practical knowledge is more than faith. Bradley, when he has followed Hegel in showing that thought develops from immediate feeling, deserts him to make the 'detached', discursive character of thought *qua* Understanding the distinctive character of thought as such. He takes thinking as it is in antithesis to sentience, and makes of it the full nature of thought. Hence he is driven to hold that thought passes into a quite incomprehensibly 'sentient' experience by a 'suicide' co-ordinate with the 'suicide' of will and of other forms of higher spiritual experience. But Bradley's absolute experience is, in the last resort, a dogma of faith. *Credit ut intelligat*, perhaps; but he cannot make and justify the transition. If you once sever the good from the intelligible, sooner or later you will find that you have divorced it also from the real.

INDEX

Synthesis, (Kant), 55, 97, 121.
— and analysis, 156.
— thesis, antithesis, and, 131.
System, 70, 74, 129, 153, 156, 158.

Teleology, 73.
— external, 26.
Terminology, philosophic, 1–3.
Theology, 45, 77, 79.
Thing-in-itself, 89, 95, 98, 101, 105, 155.
Thinking, empirical, 66, 84, 94, 120–7, 129–30, 141, 162.
— hypothetical, 121, 126, 130.
— and knowing, 113.
Thought, ch. V, 51, 80, 110–11.
— laws of, 30.
— natural history of, 82, 84, 86, 102, 120, 162, 164.
— and sense, 59–60, 65.
Time, 24–5, 47, 73, 81, 90, 95, 98, 99, 108, 110, 111, 132.
Transformation, elemental, 12, 16, 25–6.
Triad, dialectical, 131 ff., 136.
Truth, degrees of, 102, 152, 159, 160.

Understanding, xix, 65, 66, 70, 71, 74–5, 79, 81, 88, 90, 93–6, 102, 107, 111, 125, 127, 128, 129, 137, 161–3, 172–4.
Universal, 19, 34, 38, 39–40, 42, 43, 53, 84, 85, 87, 88, 89, 91, 93, 94, 107, 110.
— abstract, 96.
— concrete, 97, 100, 137, 156, 158.
— — and abstract, 94.

Value, 24, 78, 165, 167, 168, 171, 173, 174; see also Good and Judgement of Value.
Verification, 126, 148.
Vitalism, 22–3.
Vorstellung, 1, 66, 84, 167.

Wallace, W., xiii, xv, xvi.
Whitehead, vii, xi.
Will, see Activity, practical.
Wordsworth, viii.
World, the phenomenal, 87, 88, 89, 98, 101, 111.
— history, 76.

PRINTED IN GREAT BRITAIN AT THE UNIVERSITY PRESS, OXFORD
BY CHARLES BATEY, PRINTER TO THE UNIVERSITY